The Dialogical Imperative

FAITH MEETS FAITH

An Orbis Series in Interreligious Dialogue

Paul F. Knitter, General Editor

In our contemporary world, the many religions and spiritualities stand in need of greater inter-communication and cooperation. More than ever before, they must speak to, learn from, and work with each other, if they are to maintain their own vitality and contribute to a better world.

FAITH MEETS FAITH seeks to promote interreligious dialogue and cooperation by providing a forum for exchange between followers of different religious paths, making available to both the scholarly community and the general public works that will focus and give direction to this emerging encounter among the religions of the world.

Already published:

Toward A Universal Theology of Religion, Leonard Swidler, Editor
The Myth of Christian Uniqueness, John Hick and Paul F. Knitter, Editors
An Asian Theology of Liberation, Aloysius Pieris, S.J.

FAITH MEETS FAITH SERIES

The Dialogical Imperative

A Christian Reflection on Interfaith Encounter

David Lochhead

ORBIS BOOKS

Maryknoll, New York 10545

The Catholic Foreign Mission Society of America (Maryknoll) recruits and trains people for overseas missionary service. Through Orbis Books Maryknoll aims to foster the international dialogue that is essential to mission. The books published, however, reflect the opinions of their authors and are not meant to represent the official position of the society.

Copyright © 1988 by David Lochhead
Published by Orbis Books, Maryknoll, NY 10545
Manufactured in the United States of America
All Rights Reserved

Manuscript editor and indexer: Joyce Rappaport

LIBRARY OF CONGRESS
Library of Congress Cataloging-in-Publication Data

Lochhead, David.
    The dialogical imperative : a Christian reflection on interfaith
encounter / David Lochhead.
        p.   cm. — (Faith meets faith)
    Bibliography: p.
    ISBN 0-88344-612-X.   ISBN 0-88344-611-1 (pbk.)
    1. Religions—Relations.   2. Christianity and other religions.
I. Title.   II. Series.
BL410.L63 1988
261.2—dc19   88-1570
                                                        CIP

Contents

Acknowledgments

Any creative work is the product of a community as much as it is the product of an individual. These are some of the people in the community who supported me as I worked on this book:

John Berthrong is the Interfaith Officer for the Division of World Outreach of the United Church of Canada. John has persisted in telling me that what I was saying needed to be in print. He has read most of the manuscript and provided me with helpful comments, most of which I have attempted to follow.

David Chappell is a faculty member in the Department of Religion at the University of Hawaii, Manoa campus. David initially stimulated my interest in Buddhist-Christian Dialogue. He provided opportunities for me to further my acquaintance with Buddhism when I was in Hawaii during the final stages of writing this book.

Rita Gross is a faculty member in the Department of Religion at the University of Wisconsin at Eau Claire. Rita is a Vajrayana Buddhist who at various times as I was preparing this work was an important dialogue partner for me.

The Buddhist Christian Theological Encounter is a group organized by John Cobb and Masao Abe. The encouragement that I received from members of that group during its first meeting in Kailua, Hawaii, in 1984 provided the stimulus for me to think about writing about dialogue. This encouragement was reinforced by the second meeting of the group in Vancouver, B.C., in 1985. John Berthrong, David Chappell, and Rita Gross are members of this group. In addition I have been given encouragement by John Cobb, Schubert Ogden, Reginald Ray, Goshin Tokiwa, Donald Mitchell, and John Hick, often in ways of which they may not be aware.

Members of "Dharma and Gospel" are participants in an online computer dialogue in which I was involved during 1985 and 1986. I am particularly indebted to the Buddhist participants in that discussion: Mark Szpakowski of Halifax, Nova Scotia, Mike Butler of Toronto, Ontario, and Bruce Burrill of Madison, Wisconsin. I am further indebted to Mark Szpakowski for introducing me to members of the Halifax Dharmadattu during a visit there.

The Windward Council of Churches in Kailua/Kaneohe, Hawaii, invited me to serve as Theologian in Residence from January to April 1986. The ministers of the churches in the coalition joined me in a weekly discussion of the major arguments of the book. A lay group met with me for five weeks for a similar discussion. I spoke with small groups in two of the member congregations of the coalition. The responses and insights that were offered to me in these discussions were most helpful as I completed the manuscript.

The Roman Catholic-United Church Dialogue is the official "bilateral" between the Canadian Conference of Catholic Bishops and the United Church of Canada. I have been a member of that group since 1977. The peculiar nature of that dialogue has provided me with a laboratory in which many of my perceptions of dialogue have been tested, revised, and confirmed.

Pamela McBride, Donald and Heather Koots, and Tim Stevenson, students at the Vancouver School of Theology, served as research assistants during the initial stages of planning and writing.

The Macmillan Fund provided funding for research assistance and for sabbatical leave. The Anglican Church of Canada and the United Church of Canada also provided sabbatical assistance.

The Vancouver School of Theology granted me sabbatical leave from July 1985 through June 1986. Part of that sabbatical was used for the completion of this book.

My family, particularly my wife Ann, provided the at-home support that enabled me to produce this work. The experience of my children growing up in the midst of a religious diversity that is very different from my own experience of growing up in Christendom stimulated my thinking in more ways than I can adequately acknowledge. Ann has provided the stability at home that was necessary during the frequent and, at times, prolonged absences from home that my involvement in interfaith dialogue has entailed.

Introduction

Dialogue is an issue like motherhood: almost everyone is in favor of it. It is a "good thing." It is so self-evidently valid that many of us feel that we need not think about it. We tip our hats to the concept, and go about our business without a second thought.

Like many motherhood issues, dialogue is honored in our rhetoric. In our practice, however, it is questionable that we consider dialogue to be of high priority. This is particularly true of interfaith dialogue. We carry on in our religious institutions as if monologue were our chief calling. We have a message to broadcast to the world. It might be nice to have the luxury of conversations with people of other religious traditions, but we really do not have the time. The really important thing is to set about getting our message out. Interfaith dialogue is a nice idea that we might just get around to some day!

The frustration of getting churches to consider the importance of interfaith dialogue is evident in writers like Stanley Samartha and John Cobb. The agenda of mainline Christian churches in recent years has been focused on peace and justice issues, issues that go to the root of the human situation, issues that involve the very survival of human life on this planet. In the face of the urgency of the ecumenical agenda, churches regard having friendly conversations with Hindus or Muslims or Buddhists as something that will just have to wait.

The current ecumenical agenda has been influenced by the emergence in the last few decades of what has come to be called "contextual theology." This movement has recognized that the words we use to speak about God, about human nature and destiny, take on a meaning in relation to the particular context in which they are spoken. "God loves every person" has a different meaning if spoken in an affluent North American congregation than when spoken in the slums of Calcutta. Theologians have responded to this insight by attempting to integrate social analysis into their theological reflection. The differences between rich and poor, between powerful and powerless, have become important considerations in understanding how, by word and deed, the Word of God needs to be spoken today.

Contextual theology has enabled the churches to become more and more sensitive to the relevance of social and economic disparity to the way in which they understand mission. However, the economic diversity that social analysis can reveal is not the only diversity that pervades our social context. We live in a world of religious diversity as well. If, as a Christian, I need to respond in faith

1

and in practice to the presence of my neighbors, then I need to respond not only to their poverty but also to their Buddhism, or Hinduism, or whatever tradition these people represent. The problem is not with the idea of a contextual theology. The problem is that our contextual analysis has not gone far enough.

One of the factors in our relative disinterest in interfaith dialogue is, I believe, a certain capitulation by mainline Christians to secularist views of religion. Secularism assigns religion to the private realm. Public life attempts to isolate religion, defining it as a matter of private preference, as relevant to public life as the brand of deodorant you happen to prefer.

That view of religion as a matter of private preference has been reflected in the way that the churches have tended to identify the crucial questions that they are called to address in the world. But, of course, the reality is not quite that neat. Religious issues keep intruding where they are not supposed to be. A Sikh wants to wear a turban at a construction site. Catholics want public funding for their school system. Fundamentalist Islam complicates the already complicated politics of the Middle East.

This book is written from two major concerns. The first concern is that we need to pay more attention to the fact that Christians today are called to practice their faith in a world that is marked by religious diversity. The second concern is my belief that in paying attention to what is involved in interfaith dialogue, we might learn something new about what mission means in the world today.

The concern for doing theology in conscious dialogue with other religious traditions has been represented recently by a small but growing group of theologians. These include John Hick, John Cobb, Hans Küng, Stanley Samartha, Langdon Gilkey—to name a few of the more prominent representatives of this concern.

The development of a theology of religions involves attempts to recover what has been until now an invisible history. The Christian story as most of us learned it made little reference to the fact that Christian history is only a part of a world history that includes other religious traditions. There is indeed a history of Christian relationships with other faith traditions. That history, however, is largely unknown.

In studying the growing literature on interfaith relationships, I became concerned that the story was being told too simply. One is given the impression that the history of Christian interfaith relations is a simple matter of distinguishing between the "good guys" and the "bad guys." The "good guys" are those who accept people of other traditions as people of faith. The "bad guys" are those who think that people who are outside the Christian Church are ignorant of the truth.

History is not that simple. Instead of approaching the problem as one of the history of ideas, I propose that we look at the problem as one in the sociology of knowledge. What kind of theology would we expect from a community that is related in a specific way to another community of a different religious tradition? From this analysis, which is found in the first four chapters of this book, I attempt to make two main points. First, there are distinct differences between various types of Christian "exclusivism." To lump these together under the one label is not very helpful to our understanding of what interfaith relationship involves. Second, it is very dubious to assume that the bad record of Christians in relating to other religious traditions is the fault of certain Christian ideas. It is equally as likely that the bad ideas are projections of bad relationships. In short, to understand the current situation of Christianity to other faith traditions requires that we engage in ideological analysis. The problem is not exclusively, nor indeed primarily, one that can be dealt with by the criticism of traditional ideas.

I approach the subject of interfaith dialogue as one who was trained upon the borderline between philosophy of religion and systematic theology. Consequently, readers who may expect a book to be one or the other may have some difficulty in following my argument. It may seem from time to time that I jump from one to the other in mid-sentence. The explanation is that I do not see questions of conceptual clarification as separate from questions of theological substance. In this sense, the book is itself a dialogue between a philosopher who is concerned with conceptual clarity and a church theologian who is concerned with the interpretation of the Word of God in a contemporary Christian community. Both parties to that dialogue happen to be me. Three concerns—philosophical clarity, theological fidelity, and practical consequences—are interwoven as themes throughout the book.

I need to say a word about my own theological and philosophical education. Two of my philosophical and theological mentors are mentioned prominently in this work. These are Martin Buber and Karl Barth. Others are mentioned in passing: Paul Tillich and Ludwig Wittgenstein. Still others are barely mentioned at all but are very much present in their influence on the perspective that I bring to the task. The most important of these hidden mentors are Wilfred Cantwell Smith and Sören Kierkegaard.

The inclusion of Wittgenstein and Kierkegaard on this list is much more significant than might appear from the number of times their names appear in the text. Both Kierkegaard and the later Wittgenstein were philosophers of discontinuity. Their influence will be evident in my resistance to what I call a theology of partnership, the idea that there are truths that are common to all religions and that can, therefore, form the basis for interreligious dialogue. I am not philosophically inclined to recognize similarity as sameness when the contexts of similarities are as very different as they are across interfaith boundaries. The philosophical tradition that Kierkegaard and Wittgenstein represent may help some to understand an aspect of the book which might otherwise appear to be sheer perversity. I may indeed be perverse. My training, however, predisposes me to look for significance in differences.

It is important to mention my philosophical and theological lineage in order to put into perspective the approach I have taken in this work to the theology of Karl Barth. I regard Barth as one of my mentors. I have often worked out my own theological position in dialogue with relevant sections of the *Church*

Dogmatics. I do not consider myself a "Barthian" except in this sense.

What I have done here could be interpreted as an attempt to do what seems to be impossible: to articulate a Barthian theology of interfaith dialogue. That would be misleading. What I am concerned about is that the question posed by Barth about religion not be begged in a rush to embrace other religious traditions. I am in favor of the embrace. I am not in favor of begging questions.

It needs to be made clear that I am not claiming that Barth was "really" in favor of interfaith dialogue. That would be going too far. I am claiming that Barth's theology never addressed the question of interfaith dialogue and that it is not closed to it in principle. This interpretation goes against the prevailing view of Barth among those who are writing on interfaith concerns. The prevailing view holds that Barth investigated the area of interfaith relationships and erected an unambiguous "No Trespassing" sign upon it. My claim is that the whole area was one that Barth did not seriously investigate at all. To paint Barth as a xenophobe in relation to other religious traditions has become the excuse for an avoidance of the primary question that Barth poses: Are we justified by our religiosity? Barth was not an Arminian. He did not believe, as much evangelical thought believes, that we are saved by our acceptance of Christ. To ascribe to him an Arminianism that underlies this type of Christian triumphalism is a fundamental misunderstanding of his contribution to contemporary theological thought.

Having said that, I want to disavow the label "Barthian" for what I have written here. A strict Barthian would have difficulty with the importance that I give to philosophical concepts of dialogue in Plato and Buber. I attempt to show how a theology of dialogue is possible from the perspective of a protestant emphasis on the priority of revelation. I do not attempt to make that emphasis normative. My intention is quite the reverse. Some commentators suggest that a normative theology of interfaith dialogue would disqualify a Protestant emphasis from the very beginning. Against that, I want to urge that any adequate theology of dialogue must be available, in principle at least, to those of any theological conviction. An invitation to a dialogue that demands conversion to anything but dialogue itself, one suspects, must be an invitation to monologue in disguise.

1

The Ideology of Isolation

Light and Darkness

We live in a religiously plural world. That fact, in itself, is not new, nor is our knowledge of that fact new. Since earliest times, religious people have been aware that, elsewhere in the world, other people had beliefs and engaged in religious practices that were quite different from the beliefs and practices of their own communities. Christians have been aware of the existence of the Jewish community from the very beginning of Christian history. The existence of Islam was known by Christians very soon after Islam made its appearance in the Middle East in the seventh century. For centuries, Christians have known of the Eastern traditions, Hinduism and Buddhism.

Throughout most of that history, however, our knowledge of other traditions has been the product of isolation. We have known that other traditions existed, but have had little actual contact with those traditions. Consequently, Christians have known of the existence of Buddhism but have had little significant contact with Buddhists.

Part of the reason for the isolation of religions has been the hard reality of geographic isolation. For northern European or North American Christians, for example, contact with Hindu or Buddhist or Muslim communities was possible only for the few who were able to make long and arduous journeys to exotic parts of the world. Significant contact with other religious traditions was not technologically possible.

The problem of geographical isolation has been effectively overcome in the last few generations. Our technology has made the world smaller. We are able to travel quickly and comfortably to almost any place in the world. The restrictions on our mobility, where they exist, are economic or political, not technological. Through the electronic media we have the capability to communicate instantly with any place in the world. We are beginning to create communities (as, for example, through microcomputer networks) that have nothing to do with geography.

A result of these technological changes (coupled with the recent political history of the world) has been an important cultural mobility. That is to say, one does not have to go to Europe to find a European community. One does not have to go to India to find a Hindu community nor to Japan or South East Asia to find a Buddhist one. All of these communities, and others, can be found in virtually any metropolitan area of the world. In my own North American city I can find, without looking very hard, communities that are widely representative of the world's cultures and religious traditions.

Cultural and religious pluralism in our own communities leads many of us to suppose that we no longer live in a state of religious isolation. But that is not quite true. Religious isolation is not simply a function of geography. Communities that are not isolated geographically can still be socially isolated.

Consider, for example, the position of the Jewish community in Christendom. For centuries, the Jewish communities have existed at the heart of Christendom, in the major cities of Europe. Yet, even where Christians have not treated the Jewish communities with unrelenting hostility (and of hostility we will have more to say later), the relation has been one of social isolation. The Christian and Jewish communities have had as little as possible to do with one another.

Consider the attitude of the missionary movement from the eighteenth to the early twentieth century. Christian missionaries from European and North American churches were among the few, when transportation was slow and difficult, to have significant experience in countries where non-Christian traditions were dominant. Yet, the missionary ideology was one of isolation. Stephen Neill notes that at "the first really representative missionary conference of modern times," held in Liverpool in 1860, virtually nothing was said about the indigenous religious traditions of the people among whom the missionaries were working.[1] It would seem that, in the context of Western political and economic power, the missionary movement treated these traditions as the backward religions of backward peoples. The social isolation was maintained by the ideology of Western imperialism.

Consider our own experience. Many of us live and work beside people of other traditions. Yet the people whom we work beside, and whom we usually like and respect, remain complete strangers in their religious life. Secularism defines religion as a private matter. The secularism of our world has progressed to the point where we may live near or work with other people without knowing to what religious tradition, if any, they belong. Our relations with other people need not involve any knowledge of their religious identity. In the community in which I was raised, there were only Catholics, Protestants, and a few Jews. We all knew who was what. Today, my children go to school with Hindus, Shi'ite and Suni Muslims, Sikhs and Buddhists. Yet my children do not know the religious affiliation even of some of their close friends.

It may have once been true that geography was the most significant factor in the isolation of religious traditions from each other. Geography is still a factor in that isolation, but no longer is it a decisive one. It remains true that Islam has a visibility in Cairo that it does not have in Toronto. Yet one does not have to go from Toronto to Cairo to find a Muslim community. In the realm of religious pluralism, appearances can be deceiving.

Insofar as religious traditions remain isolated in the contemporary world, the roots of this isolation must be found in factors other than simple geography. These roots are complex, but two basic factors need to be identified. The first is secularism. As we have already noted, modern secular life enables us to live together with people of other religious traditions without reference to our religious identities. Urban secular life is organized so that I do not have to know, or even care, about the religious beliefs and practices of my neighbor. "Religion" has been defined by secularism as something so personal that it takes a great deal of tact for one even to ask about it.

The second factor that needs to be named as a root of the social isolation of religious traditions is the relative power that each community perceives the other to have. One of the reasons that the missionary movement, as a general rule, did not take other religious traditions seriously was because it shared the perception, created by the power of Western imperialism, that Western civilization, Western culture and Western religion were the wave of the future. This perception could not be seriously challenged until the power of Western imperialism itself was challenged. On the other hand, religious traditions that have been without alliances with the dominant powers have opted for isolation for reasons of self-defense. The Judaism of the ghetto, for example, chose to remain in isolation from the dominant Christian community because it perceived, usually correctly, that the dominant religious tradition had as its aim the abolition of Judaism.

The power relationships between communities is still a factor in the social isolation of religious communities. In the late 1950s, Will Herberg in *Protestant—Catholic—Jew*[2] argued that there was, in America, a religious establishment. There were, Herberg suggested, three "legitimate" ways of being religious in America. One could be a Protestant or a Catholic or a Jew.

Since the publication of Herberg's book, other traditions such as Islam and Buddhism have become more visibly present in North America. Nevertheless, the attitude that Herberg's work identified still exists. Religious communities such as Hindus, Sikhs, Muslims, and Buddhists tend to be regarded by the "establishment" as ethnic groups that are destined to disappear as new immigrants become assimilated to North American realities. We think of the "typical" North American as probably Christian, but possibly Jewish. The perception of the dominance of Christianity in North America reinforces the social isolation of religious traditions.

The isolated community is marked by one basic attitude. The isolated community defines reality for itself. This fact, which is basic to an understanding of the ideology of isolation, is an implication of the fundamental principles of the sociology of knowledge. The sociology of knowledge is based on the observation that the view of reality that individuals and communities share is a social construction. The ways we distinguish between true and false, between reality and unreality are defined in and by our social context. It follows that a community that is isolated from other communities is autonomous in its construction of reality. Alternative constructions of reality, which may be represented by other communities, have little or no impact on the isolated community. The community is accountable only to itself for its view of reality.

To put the point a bit more concretely, an isolated community is one in which there is a broad consensus about the way things are. What is true is what everybody knows to be true. Those who contradict what everybody knows to be true are either ignorant, deluded or liars. The isolated community is not able to take seriously the existence of other views of reality. The view of reality of the community can be successfully challenged only when the community changes, by entering into significant relationships with other communities. The view of reality is challenged when the community overcomes its isolation.

Consider an example of an isolated religious community. It could be a Roman Catholic parish in eighteenth-century Quebec, a Protestant community in nineteenth-century mid-America, a Muslim community in Saudi Arabia, a Buddhist sangha in Southeast Asia. Any isolated community of any religious tradition will do. Each of these communities "knows" that what it believes about what is ultimately real (in some communities called "God"), about the nature and purpose of human life, is the way things are. The isolated Catholic community "knows" that the Pope is the Vicar of Christ on earth. The Protestant community "knows" otherwise. The Muslim community "knows" that Mohammed is the prophet of Allah. The Buddhist community "knows" that life consists of suffering.

The isolated community may be quite aware that, elsewhere in the world, there are other communities that do not accept what it "knows" to be true. The question that needs to concern us is how the isolated community understands those other communities that do not share its construction of reality. Since the community "knows" that its own view is true, it follows that communities that do not share that view do not have knowledge. They are thus ignorant, deluded, misled, superstitious.

If the isolated community is Christian, the dismissal of other communities as "ignorant" will eventually find expression in the theology of the community. From the situation of isolation, one would expect this sense of other traditions as ignorant to be given theological justification. A theology of isolation will present Christians as those who know the truth and other communities as ignorantly waiting to hear the word of truth. One might expect the images of light and darkness to be prominent in the expression of a theology of isolation. Christ may be spoken of as the "revelation" of God with the implication that those who do not know Christ do not know God. In this connection, we might expect John 14:6–7 ("I am the way, the truth, and the life. No one comes to the Father but by me.") and similar passages to be used as scriptural justification of the theology.

The theology of isolation is readily found in the writings of spokespeople from the missionary movements of the eighteenth to early twentieth centuries. The view that the mission field was a place of both cultural and religious ignorance can be seen, for example, in the writings of William Carey in the eighteenth century. In this passage, Carey is arguing against an objection to foreign missions. The objection had appealed to the occurrence of religious ignorance at home.

It has been objected that there are multitudes in our own nation, and within our immediate spheres of action who are as ignorant as the South-Sea savages, and that therefore we have work enough at home, without going into other countries. That there are thousands in our own land as far from God as possible, I readily grant, and that this ought to excite us to ten-fold diligence in our work, and in attempts to spread divine knowledge amongst them is a certain fact; but that it ought to supercede all attempts to spread the gospel in foreign parts seems to want proof. Our own countrymen have the means of grace, and may attend on the word preached if they choose it. They have the means of knowing the truth, and faithful ministers are placed in almost every part of the land, whose spheres of action might be much extended if their congregations were but more heart and active in the cause: but with them the case is different, who have no Bible, no written language, (which many of them have not), no ministers, no good civil government, nor any of those advantages which we have. Pity therefore, humanity, and much more Christianity, call loudly for every possible exertion to introduce the gospel amongst them.[3]

The theology of isolation continues to be reflected in much of the ideology of the missionary movement even into the nineteenth century. The evangelistic mission of the Church involved the preaching of Christ as the alternative to ignorance and superstition. As recently as the publication of the *Hymnary of the United Church of Canada* in 1930, the predominant image in the missionary hymns was that of light for those in darkness:

> Can we, whose souls are lighted
>   With wisdom from on high,
> Can we to men benighted
>   The lamp of life deny?
> Salvation! O salvation!
>   The joyful sound proclaim,
> Till each remotest nation
>   Has learnt Messiah's Name.[4]

The missionary theology of isolation was supported by an ideology that defined all non-Western societies as culturally inferior. However, the sense of

European cultural, moral and religious superiority has been eroded by two world wars and the end of the great European colonial empires. The credibility of a theology of isolation, which describes other religious traditions as spheres of ignorance, has been seriously undercut.

It has not, however, been destroyed. Karl Barth was one of the first theologians to understand how the experience of the First World War had undercut the pretensions of European culture and European theology. Yet when he addresses the question of religion[5] it is the religiosity of Europe that he addresses. The non-Christian traditions remain only as shadows in the background of the discussion. The discussion is solely concerned with methodological issues in recent European theology.

The problem of how his "revelation positivism" relates to non-Christian traditions is not seriously addressed by Barth. By remaining in a provincial European context, Barth's position does not move beyond the theology of isolation in any clear way.

The provincialism of North Atlantic theology was brought into serious question by the Third World liberation theologies that began to emerge in the late 1960s. But while unmasking the cultural isolation of North Atlantic theology, liberation theology has not yet significantly broken from the religious isolation of traditional Christendom. In fact, contemporary theology, including liberation theology, has tended to present the theology of isolation in a new form.

In *Beyond Dialogue*, John Cobb[6] discusses the failure of the World Council of Churches to make a strong affirmation of interfaith dialogue. He places the blame for this failure on the dominance in the World Council of what Cobb identifies as a legacy of Barthian theology. To Barth, Cobb argues, religion was understood as simply a human activity among other human activities. What Cobb does not mention is the influence of Bonhoeffer and the "Secular Theology" of the early 1960s in the development of that idea. At the hands of the secular theologians, Bonhoeffer's call for a "religionless Christianity" led to a devaluing of religion. Not only was religion regarded as a human activity, but it was also among the least significant of human activities for Christian witness in the modern world. Secular humanity needed to be addressed in its secular activities. Reality was to be found in the marketplace. The sanctuary was a place of retreat from the world. In engaging the world, the sanctuary could be ignored.

Liberation theology[7] has tended to affirm this secularity of the world that the Gospel addresses. Working with a view of the world that sees the fundamental structures as those of power and wealth, religious diversity has not seemed fundamental to its understanding of reality. The fundamental diversity is the division of the world into rich and poor, powerful and powerless. In that description of the world, the fact that people are Muslim or Hindu or Buddhist as well as Christian does not seem to be significant.

The tendency of this emphasis in secular theology needs to be understood. If religion is treated as if it were marginal to an understanding of the world, if

religion is a retreat from reality, then religious knowledge is a form of ignorance. A secular worldview and its secular theology is no less imperialistic, no
less isolated, than the colonial worldview and its missionary theology that it
replaces.

In ignoring the religious diversity of human life, secular theologies have not
been fully consistent. If religion is, indeed, a human activity among other
human activities, then it must surely follow that the fact of religious diversity
must be included in any adequate theology of the world. The failure to include
religion within the concerns of secular theology reflects the disposition of
modern secular culture to view religion as a weakness, as pathological, as
ignorance. That is a value judgment whose roots are more ideological than they
are theological. Even Barth's application of the doctrine of total depravity to
the sphere of religion does not justify excluding the realm from our functional
understanding of what is part of "the world."

There are strong arguments in favor of the view that any Christian theology
ought to be a theology of isolation. A theology of isolation might seem to be
required by any Christian doctrine of special revelation. As long as we are
content to say that God is revealed in the natural order in a way that is open to
any rational being, it is possible to assume the universality of truth about God.
Christian theology has never been content with this view of revelation. It would
seem to require, for example, that the Incarnation was redundant, that what
God did in Jesus Christ was neither more nor less significant than what God
does in and for every human community. Christian theologians have disputed
whether there was any such thing as natural revelation. They have rarely
disputed that in Jesus Christ, God is revealed in a way that cannot be duplica-
ted by unaided reason. The special revelation that Christian faith seems to
require would seem to imply, then, that Christians know something of which
others are ignorant. Insofar as this is true, must not Christians then assume
that others live in darkness and that it is the Christian calling to help them see
the Light?

2

The Ideology of Hostility

The Other as Antichrist

The theology of isolation is possible when a community feels little threat from the other. The community is isolated, either geographically or socially, to the degree that the construction of reality of the community is not significantly challenged by an alternate view.

When, for one reason or another, a community is no longer isolated, the impact of another construction of reality is experienced as a threat. The closeness of the other and the difference of the worldview of the other calls into question the community's own understanding. The challenge of the other community is experienced as a challenge to God. It follows that the other community represents a force that is actively hostile to that which is most holy, most sacred.

The threat of the other community may be real or imagined. It may be manufactured even for political reasons. Whatever the source of the perceived threat, the theological response to the threat is clear. The other community will be described not in the relatively benign symbol of darkness but as the demonic, the enemy of God, the Antichrist.

Christian history is full of examples in which communities have felt threatened by alternative theologies and have responded by depicting their opponents as enemies of God. The early theologians described Gnosticism in these terms. Arianism was interpreted in this way by the defenders of Nicea. Islam, at the time of the Crusades, was understood as a movement against God. Catholics and Protestants, at the time of the Reformation, felt threatened by each other and described each other in these terms. Jews, while objectively not much of a threat to the dominant Christian culture in Europe, were perceived as a threat and were described as "Christ killers." Fundamentalism, a movement born out of the threat of modernity, responded by identifying "modernists" in apocalyptic terms.

The theology of hostility is not simply a Christian phenomenon. The rhetoric of hostility can be discerned right across the ideological and religious spectrum of the world. It can be found in the Islamic fundamentalism of Khomeini, and in some of the Sikh agitation for Punjabi independence. In a secular form, it can be discerned in the general media coverage of the Moonies and other so-called cults that are depicted as undermining all that is healthy in our society (e.g., the family) with the purpose of gaining power and/or wealth.

The ideology of hostility is distinguished by at least three features. First, the other must be perceived as threatening. Second, the error of the other is not understood as a matter of simple ignorance. The threatening force must be morally culpable. The other is a liar or a deceiver. Third, the other really knows the truth or is the agent of one (e.g., Satan) who knows the truth. The other community is thus perceived as engaged in deliberate warfare against the truth.

The Reformation era is a natural period in which to look for examples of the rhetoric of hostility. During this time, the religious allegiances of Europe were constantly shifting. Religious deviance was perceived as a threat to the unity of Christendom. Most religious communities thought of themselves as the potential unifiers of Christendom. In short, the existence of each community really was threatened by the others. An ideology of hostility is rarely based on simple paranoia.

In his typically "earthy" language, the writings of Martin Luther contain many examples of the rhetoric of hostility. There are few religious communities that Luther does not portray as involved in systematic hostility to God. The Papacy, Jews, "Turks," and the Anabaptist movements are all portrayed in this way. In Luther's comments on the Papacy, not surprisingly, many of the features of a theology of hostility are clearly evident.

An image that occurs frequently in the theology of hostility is that of the Antichrist. This image is used by Luther to describe the Pope. He uses the term not to claim a literal fulfillment of Biblical prophecy, but as a way of describing how he sees the Roman system as involved in making war on the Gospel:

> As a veritable Antichrist must conduct himself against Christendom, so the pope acts toward us: he persecutes us, curses us, bans us, pursues us, burns us, puts us to death. Christians need indeed to be truly baptized and right members of Christ if they are to win the victory in death over against the Antichrist.[1]

Luther's polemic is not aimed primarily against the individual person who holds the office of the papacy; nor is it directed exclusively to the office itself. He claims the whole papal church is involved with the Pope in hostility to the Gospel:

> What kind of a church is the pope's church? It is an uncertain, vacillating and tottering church. Indeed, it is a deceitful, lying church, doubting and

unbelieving, without God's Word. For the pope with his wrong keys teaches his church to doubt and to be uncertain. If it is a vacillating church, then it is not the church of faith, for the latter is founded upon a rock, and the gates of hell cannot prevail against it (Matt. 16:18). If it is not the church of faith, then it is not the Christian church, but it must be an unchristian, antichristian, and faithless church which destroys and ruins the real, holy, Christian church. So they testify here with their own mouth that the pope must be the Antichrist who takes his seat in the temple of God, being a corrupter and master in sinning, as St. Paul says in II Thess. 2 (:4).[2]

The portrayal of the Pope as Antichrist became a regular feature of Protestant militancy. In spite of the generally good relationships between Protestants and Catholics today, the image still persists in some places. The anti-Roman Catholic rhetoric of Ian Paisley, for example, continues to draw upon the images of hostility that we can find in Luther.

The threat that the Protestant reformers perceived in the Church of Rome was real enough. It is somewhat more difficult to understand the threat that lay behind the rhetoric that European Christians used in portraying Jews. Yet the same charge of active hostility to God can be seen in Luther's comments on Judaism:

Subsequently, after they have scourged, crucified, spat upon, blasphemed, and cursed God in his word, as Isaiah 8 prophesies, they pretentiously trot out their circumcision and other vain, blasphemous, invented, and meaningless works. They presume to be God's only people, to condemn all the world, and they expect that their arrogance and boasting will please God, that he should repay them with a Messiah of their own choosing and prescription. Therefore, dear Christian, be on your guard against such accursed, incorrigible people, from whom you can learn no more than to give God and his word the lie, to blaspheme, to pervert, to murder prophets, and haughtily and proudly to despise all people on earth.[3]

The ideological and theological basis of Christian anti-Semitism, in its long history, has not always been what we are describing here as "hostility." Forms of anti-Semitism have been based on ideologies of isolation and of competition. Luther's comments stand in a long tradition of Christian hostility to Judaism. It is this tradition of hostility that most clearly provided a theological support for the Holocaust.

It is difficult to portray the Judaism of the European ghetto as, in any real sense, a threat to the dominant Christian community. Yet as the "other," the strange community, Jewish communities became the scapegoat for any threat the dominant community felt but could not define. Plague, famine, or anything that it would be impious to blame on God became, at one time or other, the pretext for hostility to the Jews. The Jewish community was imagined to have a power beyond its numbers. The few rich Jews (e.g. the Jewish bankers) became the symbols of an international Jewish conspiracy that aimed to dominate the world and to suppress Christian faith.

A more recent form of the theology of hostility can be found in premillennial fundamentalism. This theology has its roots in the nineteenth-century reaction to urbanization and its accompanying liberal philosophy and theology. Premillennialism originally found its support among those groups who, in a time of change, experienced themselves as the victims rather than the agents of change. Premillennialism finds expression today among many who are not so marginalized by the events of the day. This is the dominant theology of many of the major television evangelists, including Pat Robertson of the 700 Club, Jim Bakker, formerly of the PTL Club, and Jerry Falwell of the Moral Majority. Echoes of premillennialism and its ideology of hostility inform many of the public utterances of Ronald Reagan.

Premillennialism is an eschatological doctrine that holds that Christ will return before the millenium, a one thousand year period when Christ will rule with his saints. According to most premillennialists, a time of tribulation, presided over by the Antichrist, must precede the millennial rule of Christ. Associated with the tribulation a great religious apostasy is typically expected. This apostasy, premillennialists hold, is prophesied by Daniel and by Jesus. The Whore of Babylon, in Revelation 18, is one symbol of this religious apostasy.

A strong tradition among premillennialists sees the sign of the religious apostasy in the coming together of all religions. One of the favorite candidates for the agent of this apostasy is the World Council of Churches and the "liberalism" that fundamentalists imagine the World Council to represent. The following passage is typical of a premillennialist view of the ecumenical movement:

> The first (sign of the coming apostasy) is the continuing drive for a one-world church—regardless of doctrine or even religion. If you're not "into" this sort of thing you may not be aware of the fact that a World Council of Churches exists and has as its goal the unification of all religions—Protestant, Catholic, Buddhist, Jewish—and so on.[4]

This goal of the World Council of Churches might come as a surprise to those people who work in Geneva and who, according to this author, control the Council. Nevertheless, the demonology is quite clear. The World Council of Churches in particular, and liberal Christianity in general, are associated with the spiritual Powers of these "last days" who are in active opposition to God and to the true Gospel of Jesus Christ.

Although the premillennialist movement has a long tradition of associating any religious group considered to be "modernist" with the Antichrist, the concrete focus of the premillennialist's hostility may vary. The movement, for example, is not hostile to Judaism. Premillennialists regard the establishment of the State of Israel as fulfillment of Biblical prophecy. Come Armegeddon, God will be on Israel's side and the Jews will finally accept the Lordship of Jesus Christ. If premillennialists desire the conversion of Israel, they do not consider Judaism to be a tradition in opposition to God.

Yet given the significance of Israel in premillennialist eschatology, Islam, the dominant religion of the Arab enemies of Israel, becomes a prime candidate for a new theology of hostility. Such a position is taken by Marius Baar in his book *The Unholy War.*[5] Baar is described as a missionary who lived and worked among Muslims for twenty-five years. The position he represents could be described as a Christian dispensationalist[6] Zionism that regards Islam as a system committed to opposition to the God of the Judaeo-Christian tradition.

It is not surprising that one who is as committed a supporter of Israel as is Marius Baar should be hostile to the Arab nations that surround Israel. Baar's hostility extends to Arabs as a racial group and particularly to Islam, the dominant faith among Arabs. In attempting to alarm his readers, however, Baar paints an image of an unworthy people who have gained power and wealth through the possession of oil. What emerges in Baar's portrayal is a picture of a religio-economic-political conspiracy, not unlike the conspiracy theories that are woven around the image of Jewish bankers by European anti-Semites:

> Whereas in Europe and America it has taken years of discipline and hard work to arrive at our current state of technology, it has taken the Arabs only a few years and much less work to far surpass our standard of living. The know-how comes from Europe, America, and Japan. The work force comes from the Third World. Affluence is being served to the Arabs on a silver platter. Is it any wonder they are filled with thanksgiving to Allah and are motivated to spread Islam throughout the world?[7]

> History shows that wherever Arabs have lived they have left desolation behind. I observed this personally during my years in Africa. And the West is already becoming a desert through the "blessing" of oil which has polluted our environment. Moreover, if the countries of the Middle East shut off oil they are now selling to us, it will mean the fall of the West.[8]

Baar portrays Arabs as untrustworthy, lazy people who have the power and wealth that oil brings, and he suggests that they are engaged in what turns out to be the ultimate conspiracy. Oil is the means by which Islam is to be imposed as the dominant religion of humanity.

> We have already fallen into the economic trap. Oil has brought world power to Islam, and by means of it the followers of Mohammed are seeking to bring about a global religion.[9]

In spite of Baar's evident antipathy to Arabs, his argument to this point is basically ideological. It could take the direction of a theology of isolation ("We can't let those ignorant Muslims tell us what to believe") or a theology of competition ("We Christians have a better religion. We can't let the Muslims beat us"). However, Baar develops his position explicitly as a theology of hostility. Christianity and Judaism are not merely superior to Islam as expressions of monotheism. Allah is an idol. Allah is not the same as Jehovah. Allah is a spiritual power in direct opposition to the God of Judaeo-Christian revelation.

> Mohammed . . . who came in his own name and was temporal, knew nothing of eternity and therefore accepted Satan's offer. The Islamic community is now in power because Satan is keeping his promise. We are seeing not just a clash between Christ and Mohammed, but a clash between the Christ and the spirit of antichrist.[10]

Baar, of course, expects the Antichrist to be a literal individual. His interpretation of Scripture leads him to expect that the Antichrist will come from Iraq, the historical Babylon. Nevertheless, all is prepared. The Dome of the Rock, the shrine of the Antichrist, the shrine of the religious apostasy that is destined to dominate the world, is already in place on the Temple Mount in Jerusalem.

> The temple of Israel has been replaced by a building which is ruled by the spirit of antichrist, a power which will seduce the world for a time and, if possible, even will lead astray the elect. He will offer the world riches, affluence, food, and survival. Today the call of the muezzin (the crier) is heard five times daily over the hill of Moriah: *"Allah hu akbar, Allah hu akbar"* ("Allah is the most high God").[11]

The theology of hostility, it should be noted, has substantial Biblical support. The first commandment, prohibiting Israel from having other gods before Yahweh, assumes that the worship of "other gods" is a real and dangerous possibility. The prophetic protest against the observance of Canaanite religious activities in Israel treats those activities as an affront and challenge to the God of Israel. The strict monotheism of Israel is assumed and affirmed in the New Testament. One cannot serve God and Mammon. The strange gods of the Hebrew scriptures, the "principalities and powers" of the apostolic writings, are assumed to be spiritual powers that claim human loyalty and that are in active opposition to God. One might wish to argue against someone like Baar who interprets Allah as one of the idols that are forbidden by the first commandment. One might have difficulty in arguing against Baar's hostility to Islam if we were to assume that Allah really was an idol. Monotheists do not expect to be tolerant of idolatry. The roots of a theology of hostility lie not only in ideology, but also in the logic of monotheism itself.

3

The Ideology of Competition

The Fullness of Truth

Hostility between religious communities is not as typical a relationship as popular opinion might suggest. Hostility gets all the press. When two communities live their own lives and ignore each other, that is not news. Yet isolation has probably been the most common type of relationship between religious communities for most of human history.

We hear of the hostility. When Catholics and Protestants bomb each other in Belfast, when Muslims and Christians shoot each other in the streets of Beirut, when Sikhs and Hindus attack each other in the Punjab—that's news. Hostility between religious communities is news because it is not typical. Isolation, for the most part, comes closest to defining the typical interfaith relationship. Second to isolation is competition.

A competitive relationship has two main characteristics. In the first place, competing communities implicitly acknowledge that they have some similarities. They are, so to speak, in the same business. Secondly, competitive communities place considerable stress on their differences. They stress that the ways in which "we" differ from other communities make "us" superior.

The competitive attitude is expressed in two ways. First, it is acknowledged, sometimes grudgingly, sometimes enthusiastically, that other communities are not totally outside the truth. Secondly, it is insisted, with varying degrees of arrogance, that the full truth is to be found only in the beliefs and practices of our own community.

Before Vatican II, competition was the predominating attitude between Protestants and Roman Catholics. The official position of the Roman Church can be seen as a classical expression of the theology of competition. Protestant communities were seen as heretical and schismatic. As a result of not accepting dogma as defined by the Roman magesterium and not being in communion with the Holy See, these communities were not part of the true Church.

18

Except for a few extremists, the Roman Church did not hold that Protestants were total strangers to goodness and truth. Protestants believed in Jesus Christ, even if imperfectly. They listened to scripture, even if they turned a deaf ear to the interpretation of the Scriptures by the Church. They attempted to practice the evangelical virtues of faith, hope, and love.

The official policy of the Roman Catholic Church toward relations with non-Roman churches was quite clear before Vatican II. Cooperation was possible, on a limited basis, in areas of common social service. But dialogue, in any meaningful sense, was not possible. To enter into dialogue would be to give the impression that matters of faith were negotiable. Dialogue was viewed as a form of relativism. Dialogue devalued the question of truth. One could not have a dialogue between truth and error. In matters of faith, the Roman Church could only say one thing to non-Roman communities: "You must accept the truth of our position."

Pre-Vatican II Catholicism represented a theology of competition that stopped just short of becoming a theology of hostility. During the nineteenth and early twentieth century, the Roman Church felt compelled to combat rising liberalism (and it was a liberalism that, especially in Europe, wore an anticlerical and often antireligious face) with increasingly absolutist and triumphalist claims. In its relations with more liberal movements (which is how it tended to perceive Protestantism) the sense of threat and hostility were not very far beneath the surface. Pre-Vatican II Catholicism, then, exhibited a defensive form of the theology of competition.

A more liberal form to the theology of competition tends toward becoming a theology of partnership. Both elements of the theology of competition are present. It is affirmed that there is something that "our" tradition has in common with other traditions. But it is also affirmed that the fullness of truth, in some sense, is to be found in "our" tradition alone.

The liberal form of the theology of competition can be seen in the approach of Friedrich Schleiermacher.[1] Writing early in the nineteenth century, Schleiermacher's whole theological approach attempted to ground Christian theology in an understanding of the human religious consciousness. Schleiermacher defines religion as "God consciousness," which he understands to be the universal human awareness of "absolute dependence." Human awareness of the divine started when people associated their sense of being dependent with natural objects like stones and trees. From this primitive animism, as people became more civilized and more sophisticated, they were able to dissociate their religious feelings from physical objects and to understand the unity of the source of human religious feelings, to which they gave the name "God." Humanity passed from animism to polytheism to monotheism, the highest stage in human religious development. Schleiermacher held that among the monotheistic religions, only Christianity has really transcended the lower stages of "fetishism" (animism) and polytheism. As the purest form of monotheism, Christianity represented, in Schleiermacher's view, the expression of religious experience toward which all other religions must aspire.

In terms of his time, Schleiermacher considered himself quite radical in his attitude toward other faiths. Against what he regarded as a prevailing attitude of isolation and/or hostility, Schleiermacher held that the non-Christian traditions, even the most primitive and superstitious, were genuinely rooted in the religious experience of human beings. The basic religious feeling, the consciousness of absolute dependence, was an authentic consciousness of God. Christianity did not therefore deny the religious reality of other traditions. Christianity was, however, a more adequate expression of the truth in which all religious traditions are grounded.

Schleiermacher's positive attitude to all expressions of human religion notwithstanding, there can be no escaping the fact that the position is well suited to the benign imperialism that marked the attitude of Europe toward the rest of the world during the last few centuries. If the struggle of the competitor seems missing from the tone of Schleiermacher's position, it is only because Schleiermacher sees his side as so far ahead of the competition that the outcome is not in doubt. It is the relaxed assurance of the front runner that enables Schleiermacher to be generous to the losing side. The triumphalism of the Roman Church at the time was a defensive triumphalism. It had to assert its claims against a liberalism that seemed to go from victory to victory in both political and intellectual life of nineteenth-century Europe. Schleiermacher had no such problems. He was a Christian voice for that same optimistic liberalism against which the Vatican was fighting its losing battle. Yet underneath those differences, Schleiermacher and Tridentine Catholicism share a remarkably similar position.

The competitive attitude toward other religious communities underlies almost all popular treatments of the subject by conservative Christian evangelicals that are not explicitly hostile. A typical popular evangelical work on other religions may group traditions like Hinduism, Islam and Buddhism together with "heretical" communities like Unitarianians, Jehovah's Witnesses, and Mormons. The bottom line of these discussions, no matter how fairly the other traditions are described, is that the other religious teachings fail to measure up to standards defined by evangelical orthodoxy. A common complaint is that the other traditions fail to give an adequate answer for sin. The popular evangelical works stress the differences between evangelical orthodoxy and other traditions; they also assert the superiority of the evangelical position.

Kenneth Boa's *Cults, World Religions, and You*[2] represents the kind of introduction to other religions that can be found on the shelves of evangelical bookstores. It is a popular work, directed at the reader who has little or no knowledge of other religious movements. In comparison to some polemical fundamentalist literature, Boa's work is a reasonably well-balanced presentation of the basic facts about other traditions. The work surveys the major world religions and then turns its attention to "pseudo-Christian" movements of the West (e.g., Mormonism and Unitarianism), to the occult, and to "new religions and cults" (e.g., Hare Krishna and Unification Church).

Boa's approach is not completely unsympathetic. He recognizes that no movement can have appeal without something true, something good. Nevertheless, the book assumes that other religious movements are fundamentally in competition with biblical Christianity. The evangelical Christian who wishes to encounter a representative of another religious community must take a defensive posture:

> Each religion and cult has its own distinctives. But there are a number of general biblical principles which Christians ought to apply no matter whom they encounter. The following presentation of some of these principles is based on a crucial New Testament verse: "But sanctify Christ as Lord in your hearts, always being ready to make a defense to everyone who asks you to give an account for the hope that is in you, yet with gentleness and reverence" (1 Peter 3:15).[3]

Among the principles that Boa lists is one that describes the encounter as a spiritual battle:

> This is a spiritual battle, not just a battle of knowledge or cleverness. Ephesians 6:10-18 describes the kind of armor believers should wear in this warfare. Our two offensive weapons are the Word of God and prayer.[4]

Each chapter of the book includes a brief description of the origins and beliefs of a different religious movement. This description is followed by a "Biblical Evaluation" of the position; this section focuses almost exclusively on the differences between the tradition under discussion and that which the author understands to be the true teaching of the Bible. No attempt is made to explore similarities between the biblical witness and the teachings of each tradition. Each section concludes with a summary of the things that a Christian should "keep in mind" when speaking to a representative of the other traditions. The "things to keep in mind" are generally the weak points, in Boa's estimation, of each of the traditions he discusses. Where Christianity and other religions differ, Boa's argument implies, Christianity is clearly superior to its competitors.

It is broadly assumed among evangelicals that in relation to other traditions, Christians are involved in what Carl Henry has described as "competition for souls." Consequently, although other traditions are not necessarily viewed as lacking wisdom and goodness, it is the differences that are decisive. Cooperation with other traditions and dialogue with them may be possible only within strict limits. Ultimately, however, all people are called to acknowledge Jesus Christ as Savior and Lord. Other traditions, which point humanity to other lords and saviors, can only be viewed as competitors to Christian faith.

Some motives behind the attitude of competition seem commendable but other motives are quite questionable. We live in a world, at least in North America, which is dominated by an ideology of competition in the form of consumerism. We are constantly bombarded with claims that one product is superior to all others in its class. Coke is superior to Pepsi (and vice versa!). Crest is superior to Colgate. The game of stressing the difference, of counting the consumers, never ends. The temptation is constant to play the same game in relation to religious preferences. We treat religious traditions as "brand names." We make claims for Christ or for our denominations that are indistinguishable from the claims that all advertisers make for their favorite product. We feel that Pentecostals should regard Methodists in a way similar to how Apple regards IBM. We buy into the logic of the marketplace and try to be religious by adhering to the competitive rules of consumerism.

Another motive sometimes at work in the attitude of competition is the ghost of the racism and the colonialist sense of Western superiority that is still closer to us than we like to admit. The assumption that our way is better (be it in our science, our economics, our politics, or our religion) runs very deep. The attitude that our way is a little better because it is *ours* is not altogether absent from our relations with other religious traditions.

Yet our admission that the competitive attitude can be motivated by things we would rather not admit, does not destroy the appeal of a competitive attitude. To be religious is to be committed to something one believes to be ultimate. To be Christian is to be committed to Jesus Christ. To regard God's activity in Jesus Christ as simply equivalent to ways God may have chosen to act in other religions, seems to destroy the point of the commitment. If Jesus Christ is truly "the way, the truth and the life" (John 14:6), then it is not surprising that many committed Christians feel obliged to assert the superiority of Christianity to all other traditions.

4

The Ideology of Partnership

The Universal God

Each type of relationship which can exist between a Christian and a non-Christian community can also exist between communities within Christendom. This fact is already evident in many of the examples we have chosen. Intra-Christian examples can easily be found for each of the types of relationship as well. Protestant and Orthodox communities have existed in a relationship of mutual isolation. During the Reformation, and for long afterward, Roman Catholic and Protestant communities existed in mutual hostility. The relationship between evangelical and mainline churches today is generally one of competition.

Within Christendom, what has emerged in the ecumenical movement in the last century is a theology of partnership. My own denomination, the United Church of Canada, came into being as a direct result of this movement. Before the opening of Western Canada in the late nineteenth century, Protestant churches in Canada regarded themselves as competitors. However, the effect of the missionary movement of the nineteenth century, particularly as it received concrete expression in the work of the churches on the Canadian prairies, altered the churches' perceptions of each other. Faced with the task of evangelizing in an immense geographic area with very few resources, the evangelical churches, particularly the Presbyterians and the Methodists, began to see each other as partners. Comity agreements between churches gave each denomination the responsibility for the work of the Gospel in specific localities. What mattered was that the Gospel (as understood from an evangelical Protestant perspective) was being preached. It mattered much less who was preaching it. Our common commitment to the Gospel was far more important than whatever differences existed between us.

The cooperation between churches on the mission field indicated a new perception concerning the significance of the similarities and differences among denominations. The logic of that perception, that our similarities were primary and essential while our differences were secondary and accidental, led to the next step: Church Union. The ideology of partnership found its theological expression in the motto that was adopted by the United Church of Canada: *Ut Omnes Unum Sint,* "That all may be one." The new denomination saw itself as the beginning of a historical movement in which Christ's prayer for the unity of the Church (John 17) was being fulfilled.

The United Church of Canada came into being in 1925. Since that time, there has been a backing away from church union as the inevitable result of the ecumenical movement. People are less sure that they want to risk their own ways of doing things—involving orders of service and structures of church governance—to form unions with those who do things differently. People are less sure that they want to create a super-church. They are comfortable with the more manageable size of their own denominations. They fear what bigness might do to the Church.

Yet the backing away from church union as a goal of the ecumenical movement has not resulted in a retreat from the theology of partnership. The churches of the ecumenical movement, in general, still affirm that what is in common to the churches is more fundamental than any differences that exist between them. By and large the churches share the same goal: the service of the Gospel of Jesus Christ.

That same perception of the essential unity of communities despite differences has been applied by some to all religious traditions. There are those who want to speak of the essential unity of all religions; these people claim that despite their differences, particular religions are merely different paths to the same goal. The logic of this step is parallel to the logic that has guided the ecumenical movement. It is, however, a suggestion that meets severe resistance within many religious communities.

It may be important to note that those who use the rhetoric of partnership may be motivated by some quite different concerns. In particular, there is a secular form of the ideology of partnership that functions as an excuse for avoiding the religious question altogether. To say that we all worship the same God or that all religions are basically about loving our neighbor may very well be a way of saying that religion is not important as long as people are "nice." The Roman Catholic church prior to Vatican II may have overreacted to this suggestion, but its concern about what it saw as the "indifferentism" of the ideology of partnership was not without foundation.

It does not follow, however, that all who use the rhetoric of partnership are seeking to minimize the importance of religious questions. The twentieth century has brought with it the global impact of a technological secular civilization that has put every religious tradition on the defensive. It is often argued that the common interest of the religions in resisting secularism is more important than the differences that exist between them. Although it may be difficult to define that common interest in traditions so diverse as Buddhism, Islam, and the Primal traditions, we are urged to seek that unity for the sake of the survival of religion itself.

The rhetoric of partnership is used both by those who would minimize religion and by those for whom religion is of the greatest importance. The logic may be the same. The intention is very different.

In some religious traditions, the affirmation of the essential unity of all religions is fundamental to the belief of the tradition itself. Hindus, Bahais and Unitarians are among those who would assert, in one way or another, that all religions are but differing paths to the same goal. Yet even within Christianity, often characterized as a highly exclusive tradition, there are those who would restate Christian theology in a way that would affirm the basic unity of Christianity with other traditions.

A prominent contemporary proponent of a theology of partnership is John Hick. Hick observes that, in common with Christianity, many non-Christian communities engage in the worship of a deity conceived as "the personal creator and Lord of the universe."[1] He argues that this fact must be interpreted in one of three ways: (1) There are many gods, different gods being worshipped by different religions. (2) There is one God who is worshipped by one of the traditions. The other traditions worship idols. (3) There is one God who, though conceived differently in different traditions, is worshipped by every tradition.[2]

Hick argues for the third alternative as the "most plausible" explanation for the similarities in the concept of God and in the worship of the major traditions of the world. He suggests that the founders of the major religious traditions were alike bearers of revelation from God. He characterizes as "Ptolemaic" the notion that God is specially and uniquely revealed in one particular tradition. He calls for a "Copernican revolution"[3] to recognize that it is God, not Christianity or any other particular religion, upon which the spiritual life of humanity is centered.

For Hick, this common worship of God, including and transcending all particular religions, is much more significant than all the differences between them. That does not mean, however, that Hick simply dismisses the differences or that he wishes to imagine a super religion in which all the differences would be abolished. The differences between the religions are what give the traditions flesh. Hick does not desire the extinction of diversity. On the contrary, he wants diversity to be acknowledged and valued. He does insist that the differences between religions cannot be taken as grounds to reject the validity of religions other than one's own.

Hick's position typifies a theology of partnership. All religions stand for the same basic principle: they assert the sovereignty of God over human life. They worship God. They reveal God. They mediate God's salvation to humanity. They have in common the same message, the same goal. The religions express their understanding of God in differing ways. These differences can be appreciated and valued precisely because the differences are not of the essence of each religion. The differences do not affect the validity of each religion as a mediator of the knowledge of God and of salvation.

Hick's position is not quite as tolerant as it may appear at first glance. As a member of the Christian tradition, Hick has to move against that strain in Christian theology that has been used to justify theologies of isolation, hostility, and competition. Hick concentrates on the Christological basis of "exclusivism," the idea that God is uniquely revealed in the person of Jesus Christ. He argues against a literal interpretation of what he describes as the "Myth of God Incarnate."[4] If the doctrine of the Incarnation of God in Jesus Christ can be recognized as a mythical expression of faith and not as a literal description of reality, we can appreciate that God's self-revelation in Jesus Christ is but one expression of the God who is revealed in different ways in other religious traditions.

While Hick's argument is directed against Christian exclusivism, the logic of the argument must apply to exclusivism in any religious tradition. One can follow Hick only if one is prepared to see his or her own tradition as but a single expression of God's revealing activity. This is a position that may come easily to Hindus, Bahais, and Unitarians. It is impossible for many Christians and Muslims. Ultimately Hick's position demands that representatives of differing traditions admit that their differences are not essential to their faith. That is an admission that not all traditions may be able to make.

The position that God is revealed validly and sufficiently for salvation in every tradition is an affirmation of faith. It is no less a particular faith statement than the affirmation that God is uniquely and definitively revealed in Jesus Christ or in the Qur'an. It is contrary, therefore, not only to more "exclusive" understandings of divine revelation but also to those affirmations of spirituality (e.g., Buddhist) that do not accept the centrality of a deity. It follows that not all forms of religious faith are equally valid.

When faced with a traditional exclusivism, the theology of partnership must revert to a theology of isolation, of hostility, or of competition. What are we to make of those who insist that there is no salvation apart from faith in Jesus Christ? Are people ignorant who have not yet reached our superior understanding (theology of isolation)? Hick's use of the symbol of the Ptolemaic system to characterize this position strongly suggests this attitude. Are people demonic who oppose God by confining him to a particular tradition (theology of hostility)? Or are people simply wrong if they have a real but inferior image of God that needs to be understood from the more "adequate" universalistic perspective (theology of competition)? Again, Hick's contrast of the Ptolemaic and Copernican worldviews could be interpreted in this sense.

Whatever the problems of a theology of partnership, it is based on the axiomatic affirmation that any real God must be a universal God. A God who is understood as the ground and the goal of all reality, and within reality of all human life, cannot be understood as present to and concerned with only a small segment of that reality, with a particular historical tradition. Consequently, according to the theology of partnership, the expression and affirmation of the divine in differing traditions must be understood, at least in some sense, as the expression of the activity of God in those traditions.

5

The Scope of the Typology

The attitudes of isolation, hostility, competition and partnership have both theological and ideological dimensions. The two are not identical. Neither can they be separated. Often, we might suspect, a theological stance is assumed for ideological reasons. The theological valuation of another tradition is made to justify an existing or a desired social relationship. If another community is experienced as a threat, we attribute demonic attributes to it. There are other occasions where the reverse may be true; social relationship is sought because the theology demands it.

Modern premillennialism exhibits both these tendencies. Premillennialism in its current dispensationalist forms has its roots in the conservative reaction to nineteenth-century liberalism. Much of its appeal around the turn of the century was due to its ability to interpret the threat of liberalism in apocalyptic terms. Liberal modernism could be interpreted as the apostasy associated with the coming of the Antichrist. It made theological sense of the threat that conservatives felt in the changes sweeping through European and American culture. The theology justified the desired social attitude: hostility to liberal modernism.

The theology, with its intricate interpretation of the end times, required more than simply a hostile reaction to liberalism, however. The theology required that the Jews return to Palestine and that God intervene on Israel's side at Armaggedon. According to premillennialist theology, God's covenant with Israel, which exists independently of God's covenant with the Church, will not be fulfilled until Armaggedon. At that time, Christ will appear as ruler of Israel and Israel will accept Christ as Lord.

This dispensationalist theology has led premillennialists to seek a relationship with Judaism that must be seen as essentially positive. Although they may still engage in mission to the Jews, seeking converts to Christ, premillennialists have been in the forefront of Christian support for Israel. Seeing Jews as the heirs of a covenant with God that is still in effect, premillennialists have renounced the traditional attitude of Christian hostility to Judaism. In premillennialist attitudes to Judaism there are elements of isolation (Jews do not "know" Christ), of competition (Christ is the fulfillment of Judaism), and of

27

partnership (along with Christians, Jews are a covenantal people of God).

There are, of course, ideological dimensions to the premillennialist attitude to Judaism. This is most clearly seen in the way premillennialists can be counted on to rally to the defense of the State of Israel, even in the most problematical circumstances (e.g., the Israeli invasion of Lebanon). Nevertheless, it is the theology that determines the ideology. First and foremost, the premillennialist attitude to Judaism is theologically determined. It resists ideological categorization precisely for this reason. Dispensationalism provides premillennialists with a clear theology of Judaism, and ideological commitments follow from this theology.

Rarely does a theologian or a movement treat all outside groups or traditions equally. Only an extreme sectarianism, for example, would regard *all* other religious communities as hostile to God. More typically, other communities will be assigned roles so that some communities will be regarded as lacking knowledge of reality, some will be regarded as hostile to God, some as competitors, and some, at least potentially, as allies in some aspect of mission.

A liberal Protestant, for example, may regard fundamentalists as somewhat out of touch with reality, fascists as hostile to God's purpose for the world, conservative evangelicals as competitors for the loyalty of contemporary North Americans, and secular humanists as partners in the humanization of the world. Conversely, a fundamentalist might regard various Eastern religious communities as ignorant of God, "modernists" as hostile to the Gospel, moderate evangelicals as competitors, and followers of the charismatic movement as potential partners in the work of the Gospel.

It should be clear, then, that the attitude of a religious community toward other communities cannot be simply described as "inclusive" or "exclusive." There are kinds of exclusivity, just as there are kinds of inclusivity. To understand the dynamics of how one community relates to another community, we have to ask "What kind of exclusivity/inclusivity? In relation to whom?"

It also needs to be appreciated that the attitudes described by the types are rarely found in any pure form. The same Christian work on Islam may assert that (1) Muslims are outside the light of the Gospel (isolation), that (2) Islam is fundamentally opposed to the purposes that God has revealed in Jesus Christ (hostility), that (3) the Gospel more fully speaks to the human condition than does the Qur'an (competition), and that (4) Muslims are fellow monotheists (partnership). One of the types of attitude will likely dominate the work, but all of the types may be present.

While religious apologetics are not always distinguished by consistency, this mixing of types may not be due to a lapse in logic. The differences between the types are often subtle. Isolation and hostility both see "the other" as outside the truth. The attitude of isolation assumes the ignorance of "the other" to be innocent: "the others" do not know the truth because they have not had a real chance to know it. In the attitude of hostility, by contrast, the ignorance of "the other" is not so innocent. The other community will be described as "lying" rather than as "blind."

In real and concrete examples, however, the distinction between innocence and culpability is a fine one. There is no pure innocence. Neither is there any unambiguous culpability. It is not unusual, then, to find these ambiguities reflected in religious apologetics. A common theme, in works like these, is to depict the followers of other traditions as innocent victims of the duplicity of their leaders. Thus ignorance and hostility can be attributed to the same tradition without necessarily involving the apologist in contradiction.

The attitude of competition places stress on the differences between communities. These differences may be attributed to the ignorance of the other community, or they may be attributed to more sinister motives. The attitude of competition, consequently, will carry overtones of isolation and hostility. Insofar as the attitude of competition grants some similarity between traditions, it may also carry some overtones of the attitude of partnership.

The typology of relationship that has been described here is not meant to be exhaustive. Indeed, I shall argue that a dialogical relationship, which will be discussed in later chapters is a distinct and preferable type of relationship. The types are, however, quite general, even though our interest here is primarily focused on how *religious* communities relate. The types can be applied to the relationship between any communities. Under the Reagan administration, for example, the peace movement has been regarded by the government of the United States as being out of touch with reality. The Soviet Union and its allies have been portrayed as the enemies of all that is good in the world. Conservative governments elsewhere, such as the Thatcher government in Great Britain, have been seen as partners in the foreign and economic goals of the American administration. These relationships have been given clear ideological justification by those who speak for the administration.

Because the types are general, it is not surprising that they bear striking resemblance to certain of the types defined by H. Richard Niebuhr in his classic work *Christ and Culture*.[1] Niebuhr was concerned in that work with the theology of relations between two communities: the Christian community and the secular community. Consequently, what we have considered as hostility is parallel to Niebuhr's "Christ against Culture," and what we have considered as partnership is parallel to "the Christ of Culture." What we have called competition has significant parallels to Niebuhr's "Christ above Culture."

Niebuhr's typology of Christian attitudes to culture was made possible by the fact that, within Christendom at least, the secular community and the religious community have been understood to be distinct communities. It is not that these communities are composed of different people. By and large, in Christendom, the secular community and the religious community have been coextensive. Yet the community organized as a religious community (i.e., the Church) has understood itself as a distinct society to the community organized for other purposes (i.e., the State, culture). As a result, the types of relationships which may arise between communities that are not coextensive, may arise here too. An established Church is one that is in partnership with the State. A sect defines itself in isolation from the State and from the prevailing culture.

The types have sufficient generality to be descriptive of the relations that may exist between any communities that understand themselves to be distinct. They could be illustrated by examples taken from the relations between home and school, between school and local government, or between local government and national government. In any of these areas, examples of attitudes of isolation, hostility, competition, and partnership, along with the ideologies that support those attitudes, can readily be found.

We can generalize the typology even further. There are terms—such as "culture," "philosophy," and "technology"—that refer to more than distinguishable communities. We can speak, for instance, of the relationship between "philosophy" and "religion." There are, of course, groups who can plausibly be described as "philosophical communities" and "religious communities." To speak of the relation between philosophy and religion, however, is to speak of more than just the relationship between those "communities." The relationship of which we speak includes those communities, but also transcends them. Similarly, in speaking of the relationship of religion and technology we are attempting to deal with much more than how the religious communities relate to the community of technologists. We are speaking, rather, about how abstract "powers" like philosophy, technology and religion—which pervade modern culture—are related to each other.[2]

Nevertheless, the relationship types of isolation, hostility, competition, and partnership describe ways in which these "powers" have been construed as relating to each other. Each of the types has been applied, in the long history of Christian thought, to the relationship between faith and philosophy. Each of them is applied, in one way or another, to the relationship between religion and contemporary technology. Philosophy has been portrayed as irrelevant to faith (Pascal's distinction between the god of the philosophers and the God of Abraham, Isaac, and Jacob may be recalled), as the attempt of human wisdom to overthrow the wisdom of God, as a preparation for the Gospel (Justin Martyr or Thomas Aquinas typify this approach), or as an independent avenue to divine truth. Technology, in the same way, is interpreted as neutral to (and, by implication, ignorant of) the religious quest, as a demonic power that is inherently depersonalizing, as a substitute for genuine human fulfillment, and as a means to realize God's intention for human dominion over creation.

The implication of the general nature of the types of relationships we have been discussing is this: It is not possible to separate the question of how the Christian community relates to other religious communities from the more general question of how the Christian community relates to the world. There may be questions that are unique to an interreligious dialogue. That would need to be argued. Yet even there we cannot escape the fact that there are religious dimensions to so-called secular communities and structures like the State and technology. A dialogue between Church and State is, among other things, an interreligious dialogue. A theology of interfaith dialogue, consequently, must ultimately be grounded in a theology of the world.

6

Religion and Faithfulness

The Case of Karl Barth

In the literature on interfaith dialogue, Karl Barth has often been blamed for supporting and perpetuating a negative view of non-Christian religions.[1] It is held that Barth, through his dominant position in mid-century theology, was responsible for a general disinterest, particularly by the World Council of Churches, in other religious traditions.[2]

Whatever the justice of these charges, they have often been made without a clear understanding of Barth's position. By creating caricatures of Barth, many of his critics have begged the question that Barth poses about the theological significance of religion. Barth's question has to do with the central question of the nature of truth in theology. For Barth, theological truth has to be judged by its faithfulness to the Gospel. In dealing with interfaith dialogue, Barth's question of faithfulness is one that requires an answer.

Barth deals with the question of religion in a section of the Church Dogmatics entitled "The Revelation of God as the Abolition of Religion."[3] The tone of Barth's discussion is indicated by the title of the second part of that section: "Religion as Unbelief." To understand Barth's discussion, one must appreciate the fact that, in his discussion, he is not particularly concerned with non-Christian religions at all. What he is concerned with is a particular theological procedure that determines, if one uses the procedure, what theology is really about. In this section, Barth is not attempting a comparison of Christianity with other religions. He would not have claimed any competence for that. He is concerned solely with a fundamental question that had been current for more than a century in European theology.

The procedure in question is one that went back at least to Schleiermacher and that had become popular in liberal Protestant theology. It held that certain things are fundamental to human nature, and that corresponding to these fundamental attributes are certain fundamental needs. It is part of human nature to have a body, so there are fundamental physical needs like the need for food. Higher than the physical are our emotional natures and our psychological needs. Highest of all, human beings have a religious nature and corresponding religious needs. There is something that is intrinsic to being human that can only be described as religious. Humans are, by their very nature, religious animals.

According to this approach, religions were the ways that human beings expressed the religiousness of their natures and satisfied their religious needs. As a religion, Christianity needed to be understood as the highest expression of the religious nature of humanity and the fullest answer to human religious needs.

This argument represented a way of approaching the task of doing theology. It was a method, a procedure, to guide the exposition of the content of Christian faith. The Christian teachings needed to be understood as expressions of the religious experience of humanity. These teachings could be commended as the best answer to human religious needs. Christianity could be presented as the fulfillment of the religious aspirations of all humanity.

We have already considered this approach as a type of theology of competition. Schleiermacher's formulation of the approach is one of its classical expressions. Its proponents saw it, with some justification, as a significant advance over the theologies of isolation and hostility. Nevertheless, it unconsciously reflected the arrogance of the European cultural imperialism of the time. That arrogance, that celebration of Christianity as our own achievement, was not irrelevant to the question that Barth posed.

What Barth has to say here has little to do with whether or how Christians should relate to people of non-Christian traditions. What Barth addresses is the question of the significance of "religion" for theological method. According to liberal theology, "religion" (in the sense of the innate religiousness of human nature) determines theology. Theology is the scientific expression of human religiousness. Against this, Barth holds that the task of theology is determined by the self-revelation of God. It is not determined from the human side, not even by a so-called natural capacity of humanity for religion.

Barth does not dispute the thought that humanity is naturally religious. However, he directs his critique at the implications that liberal theology tried to build on the basis of that premise. For the sake of the argument, Barth accepts the idea of the essential religiousness of human nature. He grants that in the religious achievements of humanity we can find some of the highest expressions of human greatness. What he questions, though, is whether the sublime expressions of human religiousness are the subject matter of theology. To Barth, the proper subject of theology is the Word of God. The nature and method of theology are determined by God's self-revelation in Jesus Christ, not by the human capacity for religion.

Barth is content to accept a broad definition of religion. Within his definition he would include the beliefs and practices of particular communities as well as something so abstract as Schleiermacher's definition of religion as the consciousness of absolute dependence. What all these definitions come down to, Barth argues, is an attempt to establish a relationship with God from the human side. We attempt to reach God through our beliefs and our practices or through some natural capacity that we have as humans for relationship with God.

If that is what religion is, Barth argues, then we have to understand that the Gospel places all religion under judgment. Religion is the human attempt to establish fellowship with God. The Gospel is the "good news" that God has in Jesus Christ established fellowship with humanity. In the Gospel, fellowship with God is established from God's side in spite of the incapacity of humanity for fellowship with God. Religion, therefore, is the negation of the truth of the Gospel. In attempting to establish fellowship with God, religion ignores the fact that God has already established fellowship with us. Consequently Barth draws his shocking conclusion: Religion is unbelief!

That conclusion, it needs to be stressed, applies to all religion. Christianity is not an exception. Barth is not claiming, as some critics of Barth have alleged, that Christianity is the only nonidolatrous faith. The conclusion—the judgment that religion is unbelief—is applicable first and foremost to Christian religion. To suggest that our correct beliefs, or our correct rituals, or any capacities of our own, are what brings us into special relation with God is precisely what Barth means by unbelief. To claim that what brings us into, and maintains us in, fellowship with God is something that we possess by being Christian is, Barth would claim, a denial of the Gospel.

It is not my purpose here to vindicate Barth's treatment of non-Christian religions. Barth's own relationship to non-Christian traditions I have already described as one of isolation. He shows little or no knowledge or interest in other religious traditions. In the course of his discussion of religion, he takes up the case of Pure Land Buddhism,[4] and its rejection of self-help as a way to Enlightenment. He is concerned to answer the claim made by some theologians that the doctrine of salvation by faith in the Pure Land school provides a point of contact between Christianity and Buddhism. Evangelical Protestantism and Pure Land Buddhism, it was held, have a common doctrine of salvation. Barth argues that the faith of Pure Land Buddhism is not faith in Jesus Christ, that Christian "faith" and Pure Land "faith" cannot be equated. The difference in the "object" of faith, in the one who is acknowledged as the source of grace, is decisive. In short, Christian faith exists in its witness to Jesus Christ. It does not exist to witness to a general truth of salvation by faith alone.

The point Barth is making does not depend on any familiarity on Barth's part with Pure Land Buddhism. It is a theological judgment on the nature of Christian faith, not a comparative judgment about another religious tradition. What needs to be observed here is that, in his analysis of Pure Land Buddhism, Barth is completely dependent on European scholarship. His description of Pure Land Buddhism relies on what can only be described as European stereotypes of Eastern spirituality and of the concept of Nirvana. The theological issue that Barth is addressing is an issue in European theological scholarship. Barth shows little interest in the question of other religious traditions. He seems to assume that knowledge of other religious traditions has little or nothing to do with the scientific study of the Word of God. As far as the work of theology is concerned, other traditions are not candidates as sources of Christian theology. They do not define in any way the revelation that is the task of Christian theology to serve.

This is a point that commentators on Barth often have difficulty in understanding. Alan Race, for example, tells the following anecdote:

> It has been reported that D. T. Niles, a Christian theologian from India, in conversation with Barth, once asked him how he knew that Hinduism was unbelief when he had never met any Hindus himself. Barth's reply was '*A priori*'![5]

Race takes this as an attempt "to pronounce on other faiths without a thorough prior knowledge of their beliefs and practices." What Race fails to understand is that Barth's judgment is not about Hinduism but about "Religion." It applies to Christianity as much as it does to Hinduism and has nothing to do with whether or not there are godly or saintly individuals who are Christians, Hindus, Muslims, or anything else. The point is not an empirical one but a theological judgment about ALL human activity.

Barth's discussion, I am suggesting, is set in the context of a rather provincial European theological community. There is little reason to assume that Barth did not share that provincialism. However, the provincialism being granted, the serious questions that are raised by Barth still stand.

Barth clearly dissociates himself from those who see other religions, or religion in general, as a preparation for the Gospel. The argument he wishes to challenge holds that there is a universal essence of religion. Christianity, the argument holds, measures up to that essence better than any other religion. Barth describes this argument, which he traces beyond Schleiermacher to the seventeenth-century theologians Buddeus and van Til, as the reversal of the insistence of the Reformation on a "religion of revelation" to a newly discovered "revelation of religion."[6]

Barth's conclusion that religion is unbelief is primarily directed against the position that Christianity is the fulfillment of religion, and that human religion in general should be viewed as a preparation for the Gospel. His objection is that to take human religion as the "given," as the starting point of theological reflection, is to be unfaithful to that which is truly "given" as the basis of theology, namely God's self-revelation in Jesus Christ.

In terms of our categories of isolation, hostility, competition and partnership, Barth's critique is directed primarily against the theology of competition. It will be clear, however, that the critique would be equally applicable to a theology of partnership. In naming Jesus Christ as the one in whom God is definitively revealed, Barth makes it impossible to assert that what all religions have in common is more significant than any differences between them.

From his critique of religion, Barth goes on to speak of the Christian religion as the true religion. In spite of the use of the definite article ("*the* true religion")[7] here, Barth is not attempting to assert the superiority of Christianity qua religion over other religions. Rather, he is attempting to articulate a theme that appears and reappears wherever a theologian has to speak of the human reception of grace. Thus, Barth insists, we can speak of a "true religion" only in the same sense as one can speak of a "justified sinner."

This theme can be illustrated if we think about the doctrine of the Church, a doctrine that closely parallels what Barth says about religion. The Church is a human institution in space and time. It exists in the world as an institution among other institutions. It can be described in the same sociological terms that we would use to describe any other human institution. Yet thinking theologically, we have to believe that God, through the Holy Spirit, really does bring into being the human community in which God's sovereignty is really acknowledged and in which God's grace is received. The community which is established by the initiative of God is "Church."

The problem, a perennial problem in theology, is how to understand the relation of Church and church. If we identify the empirical institution with the divine reality, we end up with a kind of triumphalism that is blind to the realities of sociological relativity that apply to all human institutions. We deny, in effect, the genuine humanity of the church. If we divorce the two, we assert that the true Church is always invisible, and we effectively deny the reality of the Church. A community that never becomes visible is no community at all.

Barth's treatment of true religion deals with just this tension, although with a somewhat different focus. Religion is a human activity that involves all the relativity and ambiguity that human activity is heir to. Religion is, Barth suggests, the human activity par excellence. Revelation is God's activity. In revelation, God establishes God's sovereignty over human beings. Revelation, Barth asserts, is real. God's sovereignty really does "take flesh." Furthermore, it "takes flesh" precisely in the sphere of human activity that we call "religion."

In answer to the question of where in the sphere of human religion God's revelation takes flesh, Barth answers "in the Christian religion." This is not to say that the Christian religion is the content of revelation. Barth's claim is not that Christianity is a revealed religion. Rather Barth's claim is that Christianity is the locus of God's self-revelation, of God being really known by human beings, of human beings really entering into fellowship with God. In short, Barth is not attempting to assert triumphalistically the superiority of Christianity over other religions. He is attempting to maintain that there is a genuine response to God through the Gospel of Jesus Christ within the religious tradition we know as Christianity.

If true religion is the genuine reception of and response to God's self-revelation, the question remains as to whether traditions outside Christianity can be the loci of true religion. Is Christianity the only religion within which there is a genuine hearing of and response to the Word of God? Even granting Barth's criticism of religion, can we not assume that God has not abandoned the non-Christian world, that a genuine knowing God and fellowship with God occurs, by God's grace, in Hinduism or Islam as well as in Christianity?

On this point, Barth is virtually silent. On relatively weak evidence, Barth is usually understood to confine true religion to Christianity. As we shall see, there is other evidence that Barth did not confine the revealing, redeeming, and reconciling activity of God to the Christian religion. Whichever way we interpret Barth, the fact remains that on this point Barth was very cautious and tentative. We need to understand the reasons for his caution.

The question that concerns Barth here is how we would recognize the activity of God in other religions. By what criteria can we recognize revelation? What is involved here is the question of the ultimate criteria of theology. How do we test the spirits to see if they be of God? The answer to this question, according to Barth is that the spirits are tested by Christological criteria. We know that the spirits are of God if, and only if, the spirits witness to Jesus Christ.

Barth is claiming, in effect, that Jesus Christ is God's self-identification, God's self-definition. It is not that Jesus Christ is one revelation of God alongside other revelations. Rather, Jesus Christ is the paradigmatic revelation. God is the God who is revealed in Jesus Christ. All our language about God, all our religious experience, is accountable to the ultimate criterion of the self-revelation of God in Jesus Christ.

Of course, other criteria of revelation are possible. We can identify God, following Schleiermacher, as the "Whence" of our consciousness of absolute dependence. We can identify God as the creative force we intuit in all of nature. We can identify God as the power of human love. To do that is to have different ultimate criteria, different paradigms of God's self-revelation.

What is at stake here, for Barth, is the accountability of the theologian to the first commandment: "Thou shalt have no other gods before me."⁸ The question put to theology by the first commandment is the question of the ultimate authority, the ultimate criterion for theological thought and speech. A theology confesses its faith in and through the ultimate authorities to which it appeals.

Suppose we were to ask whether Islam, like Christianity, can become, through the grace of God, the locus of true religion. The question implied by Barth's analysis is how we would know if it were so. We can appeal to the fact that Allah, the God of Islam, is, like the God of Christian faith, a single personal deity. Yet Satan is single and personal too. The similarity of the way in which we describe our deities does not establish their identity.⁹ Put another way, our concept of God is not our ultimate criterion of God. Christians do not start out with an idea of God which they find that Jesus lives up to. They start with the life, death, and resurrection of Jesus Christ and discover through revelation what God is like. Similarly the Muslim starts with the Qur'an as the revelation of Allah and discovers through the Qur'an how to think and speak about Allah.

One could try a different tack and try to compare the religious experience of Christians and Muslims, or the examples of high spirituality that can be found in both traditions. That too would beg the question, unless we were to say that religious experience and/or human spirituality were the ultimate criteria in recognizing and identifying the presence of God. If God be God, Barth needs to insist, God sets the ultimate criteria. The Christian theologian has no option but to accept the criteria that God sets by taking flesh in Jesus Christ. To be Christian rather than Muslim is to look to Jesus Christ, rather than the Qur'an, as God's setting of the criteria.

The argument is, of course, circular. The option for Barth is quite simple. Either we are faithful to the particular criteria that are given to us in our particular tradition, or we say that there are criteria that are higher than the criteria of particular traditions. If we have higher criteria—a knowledge of God that transcends the self-revelation of God in Jesus Christ—that judge and authenticate that revelation, then we do not really need Jesus Christ. If there can be a higher criterion for the Muslim than the Qur'an, then the Muslim really does not need the Qur'an. If Christians persist in finding God in Jesus and the Muslims find God in the Qur'an, it is basically for sentimental reasons. Our real faith is in our higher criteria.

It can be fairly said of Barth that his argument begs the question of criteria: one acknowledges Jesus Christ as the ultimate authority for thinking and speaking about God because that is the way God chooses to be known. But one believes that is the way God chooses to be known because one acknowledges Jesus Christ as the self-revelation of God. It is arbitrary and circular, because ultimate criteria are always arbitrary and circular. If they were not arbitrary and circular they would not be ultimate. What Barth shows is that, when it comes to the revelation of God, there are no criteria that do not beg the question.[10]

Barth's position is not what it is often confused as being: Christian triumphalism. The critique of religion is first and foremost what Barth said it was: a critique of Christian religion. It is a critique of human religiosity that has the Christian expression of that religiosity foremost in its mind.

Barth's critique of religion is a defense of the free sovereignty of God. It is fundamentally concerned with God's freedom to be God. But if the point is put that way, another question must inevitably arise. If God is free and sovereign, then is not God free to be present to human beings as revealer, redeemer, and reconciler, outside the sphere of Christian religion?

The answer is that God is indeed free to reveal, redeem, and reconcile outside the sphere of Christian religion. In a section that is usually unnoticed in this connection, Barth raises the question of words of God that are spoken outside the sphere of Bible and Church. The sovereign activity of God, Barth insists, cannot be confined to Christian religion.

> If with the prophets and apostles we have our starting-point at His resurrection and therefore at His revelation as the One who was and is and will be; if we recognise and confess Him as the One who was and is and will be, then we recognise and confess that not we alone, nor the community which following the prophets and apostles, believes in Him and loves Him and hopes in Him, but *de iure* all men and all creation

derive from His cross, from the reconciliation accomplished in Him, and are ordained to be the theatre of His glory and therefore the recipients and bearers of His Word.[11]

If genuine words of God are to be recognized outside the sphere of Bible and of Church, Barth argues, certain criteria need to be met. There are signs by which the Christian community can recognize, if tentatively, the Word of God in words that have their origin in the world outside the Christian religion. There are four criteria which Barth names.

First, the word that comes from the world, if it is a genuine word of God, will cohere with the witness of scripture. That is not to say that outside of scripture we have nothing new to learn or that we must be able to "proof text" any claim to have heard God speak in the world. It does mean that the word that is heard in the world will not distract us from the word of scripture, but will enable us to hear scripture in a deeper way.

> Wherever we seem to have a true word in some phenomenon of nearer or more distant occurrence, we must always ask concerning it agreement with the witness of Scripture. Naturally, we cannot expect that in its concrete form it will be anticipated and therefore confirmed in a biblical text or passage. But we should expect that, if it is a true word, its message will harmonise at some point with the whole context of the biblical message as centrally determined and characterised by Jesus Christ, that when it is compared with this it will not disturb or disrupt its general line but rather illuminate it in a new way at some particular point.[12]

Secondly, the worldly word will be in continuity with the confessional tradition of the Church. It will not contradict the classical confessions, although it may well teach us something that was not known to those who framed the creeds and confessions.

> With certain qualifications we must also consider the relationship of these other words to the dogmas and confessions of the Church as a criterion of their truth. . . . If they are true words, they will not lead us away from, but more deeply into, the *communio sanctorum* of all ages which is attested in these documents. If they lead to a breach with them, they will show themselves to be false words. But it may well be that the Christian community, assuming that it hears such true words here and now, has still new things to hear and learn which go beyond its dogmas and confessions and which the fathers and brethren could not teach it in the days when these documents were formulated. If these new things, and therefore the truth of these words, are authentic, it may well be expected that their light will somehow be an extension of the line visible in the dogmas and confessions, so that they supplement even though they do not contradict what is stated by them.[13]

Thirdly, the word that is spoken outside the Bible and the Church must be judged by its fruits in the context in which it is spoken. Does it enhance humanity or devalue it? Does it create hope or destroy it? The word that is genuinely spoken by God may be expected to bring forth fruits that are consistent with the Gospel.

Finally, the word may be judged by the effect that it has on the Christian community itself.

> . . . these other words may be recognised as true words by what they signify for the life of the community itself, for its activity under the special command and promise of its Lord. . . . they will have for it in indissoluble unity the character of affirmation and criticism, of address and claim, of a summons to faith and a call to repentance, and therefore of Gospel and Law.[14]

Barth makes this point very strongly. As long as the critique that is heard from the world is not destructive and disabling, he implies, a word that calls the Church to repentance can be trusted as a word from the Lord.

Barth calls those words that are spoken by God outside the Bible and Church "secular parables of the kingdom." In the whole discussion, Barth barely alludes to non-Christian religious traditions. He has the world of secular humanity, the world of the militant secularist and of the nominal Christian primarily in mind. Again we are dealing with a European theologian speaking in the context of a European world. Yet the question and the criteria are clearly applicable to other religious traditions. In other traditions we do hear words that complement rather than contradict the Biblical witness and the confessional tradition of the Church. We do see those words bringing forth fruit that is consistent with the Gospel. We do hear words that call us, as Christians, to repentance. Barth's theology, in spite of Barth's isolation, does affirm the possibility of the presence of God in other traditions.

The theology of Karl Barth, in spite of what many critics have claimed, is not a theology that is closed to dialogue with communities of other traditions. In principle, it is a theology that is open to and affirming of *any* dialogue with the world. The question Barth puts is whether the proposed dialogue is a faithful one. If we beg the question of faithfulness, Barth warns, we may be engaging not in a dialogue, but simply in a monologue with liberals of many faiths.

7

Faithful Agnosticism

The relationships, which I have distinguished by the terms isolation, hostility, competition, and partnership, are not intended to exhaust the possible attitudes that may exist between religious communities. These are the relationships that have informed the theological attitudes that have dominated Christian understandings of other religious traditions in the past. These relationships have been reflected in theology. Theology has legitimized these relationships.

The ideological role of theology is not surprising in this context. Clearly, a Christian community can enter a new relationship with another religious community only insofar as the new relationship can be construed as a form of faithfulness. In attempting to argue for a different, more appropriate understanding of other religious traditions, theological work has to run counter to traditional models of faithfulness that have been formed by relationships of isolation, hostility, competition, and partnership. Some of these traditional models may seem basic to Christian faith, especially when the proposed partner in dialogue represents a non-Christian tradition.

The theology that supported a relationship of isolation suggested that God's unique and ultimate revelation was to be found in Jesus Christ. Those who did not know Jesus Christ, consequently, were considered to be ignorant of the true God. To move against this model, to suggest that the relation between Christian communities and non-Christian communities is something other than the relationship between light and darkness, seems to be to suggest that the revelation in Jesus Christ is not unique and ultimate but relative and partial. To question the uniqueness and ultimacy of God's revelation in Jesus Christ, it seems, is to be something less than faithful. Faithfulness would seem to require that we see other traditions as fundamentally ignorant and superstitious.

The relationship of hostility and the theology that legitimizes it also has strong Biblical roots. The very logic of Hebrew faith, as we know it through the Hebrew scriptures, relied on a sharp distinction between the God of the Patriarchs and the Exodus on the one hand and, on the other, the "other gods" which were worshipped by the "nations" in general and the Canaanites in

40

particular. Faithfulness, in the apostolic writings as well as in the Hebrew scriptures, involved faithfulness to the God who is known through the Prophets and Gospels as opposed to the many gods and lords of surrounding communities. Openness to other traditions, in this light, would seem to be openness to idolatry. Faithfulness would seem to require a relationship of hostility to communities of other religious traditions.

In the development of the Christian tradition, a heavy emphasis came to be placed on credal orthodoxy. The particulars of this development need not be repeated here. The result of this emphasis has been that any movement that tried to relativize credal orthodoxy has been perceived as potentially schismatic. To belong to the Christian Church, for many, involves loyalty to the basic doctrines of the Church as defined by Councils and in Confessions. To fail to defend these definitions, to fail to insist on their nonnegotiable character, as required in a competitive relationship with other traditions, implies a failure to be faithful to the guidance of the Church by the Holy Spirit.

The theology of partnership, while apparently vulnerable to these charges of infidelity, can level some charges of its own. To fail to see that God is revealed in all creation, and therefore in each and every religious tradition, makes one seem less than faithful to the universality and transcendence of God. To fail to affirm that God is revealed in all religions makes one seem faithless to the kind of tolerance we discern in the example of Jesus and to the kind of humility he modeled for us.

Each of the ways that theology has tended to legitimize particular forms of relationship with other religious communities is subject to its own critique. I do not propose to focus on particular criticisms of any one of these types. All four, I want to argue, are subject to a common criticism, and it is on this criticism that I wish to concentrate.

The theologies of isolation, hostility, competition, and partnership all depend on an a priori valuation of other religious traditions. That is to say, each of the theologies makes a decision about the validity or authenticity of the other religious traditions in abstraction from actual dialogue. In the theology of isolation, other traditions are "known" to be spheres of ignorance and superstition quite independently of any knowledge of the tradition. At the other end of the scale, other traditions are "known" by the theology of partnership to be locii of divine revelation even though, as in the case of Buddhism, the very concept of God may be problematic for the tradition. The theology of competition may seem to be least vulnerable to this criticism, but even here other traditions are assumed to be competitors that will corrupt the pure Gospel if given a chance. They are assumed to be poor imitators of the Truth that is known in our own tradition.

The theological question that has to be raised around the question of faithfulness to the Gospel in our relationship with other religious traditions is this: Does the Gospel require a prior valuation of a tradition with which we enter into dialogue? Must we "know" the place of another tradition in God's scheme of things before we can faithfully risk a conversation with that tradition? Must our relationship with other religious traditions be determined a priori?

There are many legitimate nontheological reasons for rejecting the a priori approach. Our empirical prejudices would require that valuation follow from evidence rather than precede it. It should be clear from the variety of traditions that exist in the world that no single valuation will cover every case. I would agree with the contention that our understanding of other traditions should be based on at least a minimal conformity to scientific norms. Conformity to empirical method, however, does not resolve the theological question of faithfulness.

What then does the Gospel require of us in our relations with other traditions? Does the Gospel require an a priori valuation of other traditions?

I would argue that in one case the Gospel does require an a priori valuation: the case of Judaism. There is no way that, in faithfulness to the Gospel, the revelatory character of the basis of Judaism can be denied. The question of the faithfulness of the Jewish community to its basis can be raised, but only in precisely the same sense that the question of the faithfulness of the Christian community to its basis must also be raised. In other words, the Gospel does require an a priori valuation of the Jewish tradition and, insofar as the valuation is a priori, it is a positive valuation.

Christians believe that the validity of Christianity depends on the fact that "God was in Christ." The validity or truth of Christianity does not depend on the quality of Christian discipleship, of the success of Christians in being faithful to what the Gospel calls them. The Christian record in saintliness is not particularly impressive; few, if any, would argue for the truth of Christianity on those grounds.

Yet when it comes to Judaism, Christians have tended to dismiss Judaism on the grounds of a supposed faithlessness of the Jewish people. This disregards the fact that the Christian record for faithfulness is no better. It also disregards the fact that, if "God was in Christ," then it is also true that God spoke and speaks through the patriarchs and prophets. In short, if Christianity is "true" because it is God-initiated, the same *must* be true for Judaism. As a matter of Christian faith, the validity of Judaism is given a priori. If Judaism is not of God, then neither is Christianity.

I would stop there, however. In no other case can an evaluation of another tradition be a priori. The Gospel could be said to require a rejection of idolatrous religions of the Canaanite type. However, the Gospel does not give us the grounds that we would need to identify a priori a living religious tradition with the Canaanite type of idolatry. That judgment, if it is to be made at all, is a judgment that requires the evidence of experience.

It is the Canaanite paradigm that gives us the most difficulty. It has been used indiscriminately in the past. It was the Canaanite paradigm that made missionaries on the North American frontier willing collaborators in the suppression of native culture by the white community. It is the Canaanite paradigm, applied with much more subtlety, that lies behind Barth's judgment that religion is unbelief.

Barth's point, as we have already seen, is that the gods are the ultimate criteria of reality to which human beings appeal. To have different ultimate criteria than the self-revelation of God in Jesus Christ is to have "other gods." That, Barth argues, is precisely what is forbidden in the first commandment. The gods of the other traditions are idols, or so it might seem.

It is one thing to acknowledge that idolatry is incompatible with Christian faith. It is quite another thing to identify a particular belief or practice as being idolatrous. The question is not whether Christians can be neutral about idolatry. The question is how we can recognize an idol when we see one.

One of the things that often goes unnoticed in discussions of idolatry is the fact that the concept of idolatry has its force primarily *within* the Judaeo-Christian tradition and only secondarily in direct reference to other traditions. When Barth and Tillich, for example, speak of idolatry, they are referring to the functional gods of Christians, the "ultimate concerns" that Christians serve, in practice, before the God of the Gospel. Only rarely, in contemporary theological discussion, is idolatry used to refer to the beliefs and practices of non-Christian traditions.

The modern use of the concept of idolatry is not an innovation, however. A similar observation could be made of the Biblical texts themselves. The problem of the Canaanite is not that Canaanites worship badly. The problem is that Israel might be seduced into practices borrowed from the Canaanites—and *that* would be idolatry!

Consider the story of Elijah and the priests of Baal (I Kings 18). Elijah stages a contest between Yahweh and Baal on Mount Carmel. The contest is won by Yahweh, whose divinity is thus proven. Baal, the loser of the contest, is exposed as an idol. As a result, the prophets of Baal are all killed at Elijah's command. This story illustrates in a dramatic way the "theology of hostility" that can be found when the Bible deals with idolatry.

The problem, for Elijah, is not that the worship of Baal exists. The problem is that it is being imported into Israel as part of the royal cult. Whether it is idolatry for Canaanites to worship Baal is a question about which the Hebrew Scriptures show very little interest. What is clear is that it would be idolatry for *Israel* to worship Baal. It was precisely this threat that the policy of Ahab and Jezebel, in promoting the cult of Baal, posed for Israel. It was this policy that Elijah and other prophets so vigorously opposed.

There is a crucial distinction here that probably would have made no sense to the Hebrew prophets but that is necessary for us. Idolatry poses two questions: Is Baal an idol? Would it be idolatry for me to worship Baal? To the prophets, especially prior to the Exile, those would probably be identical questions. But the prophets assumed that Baal exists! To be an idol in any objective sense, the idol has to exist as a being who is involved in direct competition with God. If Baal does not exist, then the worship of Baal is not so much idolatry as it is ignorance.

The distinction between the objective existence of an idol and the practice of idolatry is crucial for us. For our problem is *not* whether Allah exists in competition with the God of the Gospel or whether Allah is the same being as the God of the Gospel or whether Allah exists at all. Indeed, it is difficult to know how we could even begin to make sense of those questions. Our problem is what we are to make of the fact that Allah is worshipped. Do we deplore this or celebrate it? Could we, as Christians, worship God using the name "Allah"?

From time to time I have been in Buddhist shrine rooms in order to meditate. I enter and sit and meditate in a manner consistent with the fact that I understand myself to be Christian rather than Buddhist. I observe Buddhists who enter the room and who face a statue of the Buddha and bow before they sit. What the Buddhists are doing is not something that could be described as "idolatry." After all, Buddhists do not believe in any deities, let alone false ones. The bow, I am told, is an act of reverence to the "Buddha nature," the potential for enlightenment that is in all being.

The problem is that bowing to a statue of the Buddha could not mean that for me. For a Christian, the behavior of bowing before an image has a meaning that is embedded in the very center of the Christian tradition. In the syntax of Christian worship, bowing before a Buddha statue comes too close to idolatry for comfort. What is not idolatry in Buddhist categories could be idolatry if attempted by a Christian.[1]

Wilfred Cantwell Smith has often made the point that the animist worships the stone that the animist sees, not the stone that the Christian sees. That point is a crucial one. Whether a Hindu or a native shaman is involved in idolatry is not something that I can judge in any a priori and absolute way. At most, I can say that their practices are not something I can imitate without raising the question of idolatry for me.[2]

The conclusion that I draw from these considerations is that the Gospel, except in the case of Judaism, provides no warrant for an a priori valuation of other traditions. In relationship to the integrity or truth claims of other traditions, the faithful attitude is one of agnosticism. Discipleship to Jesus Christ does not require of us either a rejection or acceptance of the claims of other traditions. Openness to the world, which we understand as the arena of God's activity and as the object of God's love, requires of us that we listen.

The refusal to make a priori valuations of other traditions is by no means a refusal to acknowledge that there are moments of grace—of revelation and salvation within other religious traditions. When Karl Rahner[3] argues that other religions are arenas of salvation, he is claiming that we can expect to find signs of God's activity in our encounter with other religious traditions. On this point, Rahner is surely correct. When he claims that other traditions are in this sense salvific, his argument is more difficult to accept. There may have been moments of grace in Jonestown. But to argue on that account that Jonestown has positive significance in God's economy of salvation stretches the concept of positive significance to the point of meaninglessness. Theologically, there is no difficulty in affirming the presence of God in other religious traditions. There is no theological basis, however, for making global judgments about specific traditions on those grounds.

It is important that we be clear about this. We are in danger of justifying dialogue on the basis of an idealization of other traditions, of Hinduism and Buddhism, of Judaism and Islam, of native spiritualities. We are in danger of justifying dialogue on the basis of an a priori positive valuation of other traditions. Against that temptation, we need to remind ourselves that the world of religious pluralism encompasses Jonestown as well. A dialogical stance will have to include racist churches in southern Africa, the Unification Church, the Moral Majority, the Jehovah's Witnesses. We need to remind ourselves that every tradition, including our own, has its dark side as well as its light. In the past, we may have been too prone to see the darkness in others and too resistant to seeing the darkness in ourselves. We gain nothing if our vision is reversed, if in the name of justice and tolerance we become too prone to see our own darkness and too resistant to see the darkness in others.

The agnosticism that I am suggesting is proper to faithfulness is an agnosticism that is prior to dialogue. In dialogue, judgments will have to be made. In dialogue, we encounter the principalities and powers, forces and ideologies that are the denial of any Christian vision of the meaning of human life in God's world. In these cases, the powers will have to be named. Hostility to the threat to our common humanity will be a faithful response to the Gospel. In other cases, we will discover the fruit of the Spirit in the midst of other religious traditions. In those cases, a positive response to what we find elsewhere will be appropriate.[4] When we believe that we discern the work of God's Spirit, that too should be named. We name, tentatively yet firmly, the signs of the principalities and powers as well as the signs of the Spirit. We have no warrant to baptize those who do not wish baptism. We do have a warrant to discern the spirits.

8

Two Philosophers of Dialogue

"Dialogue" is both an old word and a new word. In the Western intellectual tradition, "dialogue" has roots in the Platonic tradition. There it refers to a method. In Plato's dialogues, Socrates is portrayed as one who uses a method of question and answer; through dialogue, he hopes to arrive at a better understanding of truth. The concept of dialogue, then, has a distinguished and ancient intellectual pedigree.

In theological discussion, dialogue is quite a new word. In the *Religious Index to Periodical Literature*, for example, the word appears as a subject heading only in the mid 1960s. This, not quite coincidentally, is contemporary with Vatican II. The entry of the Roman Catholic Church, under John XXIII, into the mainstream of ecumenical discussion stimulated discussion of how traditions, long alienated, could come to understand and appreciate each other. "Dialogue" became the key concept in this discussion. In the later 1960s and the 1970s, the word increasingly became applied to interfaith relationships. It was used in the name of the program of the World Council of Churches that was concerned with interfaith relationships: Dialogue with People of Living Faiths and Ideologies.

In the context of interfaith relationships, then, we are attempting to use an old word in a new setting. In the new context, the word "dialogue" does not have a fixed meaning. In the dialogue about dialogue, some commentators draw on the rich, if somewhat invisible, history of the concept in the Western intellectual tradition. Others understand the concept more literally as "conversation" and suggest that dialogue is only an initial step in the development of positive relations between the religious traditions of the world.

The word "dialogue" is used here in the broader sense. The concept of dialogue, I will argue, is rich enough not only to support a theology of interfaith relations, but to support a theology of mission as well. The word "dialogue" names the fundamental attitude with which the Church is called to encounter the world. It follows that there is no need to move "beyond dialogue." In this sense, dialogue is an end in itself. In this chapter I want to prepare the way by looking at two important resources for thinking about dialogue: Plato and Martin Buber.

THE PLATONIC LEGACY

In Plato, dialogue is a method for conducting a search for truth. In the Dialogues, Socrates appears as one who makes no claim to knowledge but who, through entering into conversation with others, exposes the falsity of what we think we know and, through question and answer, leads us into a deeper understanding of truth.

Dialogue, as practiced by Socrates, is an art. There is no naïve belief in Plato that truth automatically emerges when two people converse together in a spirit of openness. Plato presents Socrates as a master of the art of asking questions. The questions posed by Socrates transform the conversation into dialogue. The questions enable the truth to emerge.

The Socratic method of dialogue, however, makes assumptions that have given Christian thinkers some difficulty. A paradigm of the Socratic method is the conversation between Socrates and the slave boy in *Meno*. By a process of only asking questions, Socrates leads the boy to a knowledge of a geometrical proposition that the boy was not able to recognize at the beginning of the conversation. The conclusion that Socrates draws from this example is that, because Socrates did not tell the boy the truth but only asked questions, the truth had to be "in" the boy, albeit in a forgotten form. Learning, for Socrates, is a remembering of a truth that is already in us. The educator, through the art of dialogue, enables the truth to emerge.

Supporting this dialogic philosophy of education is Plato's idealistic metaphysic. For Plato, truth lies in the realm of the universal, the abstract, the rational. What is genuinely real, genuinely true, are the universal ideals: Goodness, Beauty, and Truth. The concrete, the particular, and the empirical are only imperfect expressions of universal realities. Justice itself always transcends any particular just act. The real world, the world of universals, is not the empirical world, the world of appearance. According to Plato, we know the real world prior to birth. Birth is a forgetting and dialogue is the method by which we remember forgotten truth.

The presuppositions of the Socratic method have raised many problems for Christian thinkers. The central tension that concerns us here involves the question of the source of truth. Is truth something that we have within us, waiting to be appropriated by the proper method? Or is truth something that is external to us, that must come to us, if it comes at all, by some kind of revelation? This is the question that is put in a brilliantly pointed way by Kierkegaard's pseudonym Johannes Climacus in *Philosophical Fragments*. Climacus suggests that in this point, Christianity differs fundamentally from Platonism and that Christ "teaches" (i.e., communicates the truth) in a fundamentally different way than does Socrates. Christ communicates a truth that is not already "in" the learner in a forgotten or potential way.

The assumption that truth comes through revelation has not inclined Christian thinkers to look to dialogue as a source of truth. Rather, truth has been sought from without, through the scriptures and through the natural world. Even where Christians have understood truth to be immanent to the soul, either by virtue of its created goodness (the image of God) or by virtue of the indwelling of the Holy Spirit, the way to truth has been seen as prayer, meditation, reflection, or introspection, not as dialogue.

The traditional Christian response to Platonic philosophy has taken two forms, then. On the one side are those who have tended to reject any notions of innate truth and to articulate a theology of revelation. On the other side are those who recognize in human nature some innate capacity for the truth and, through reason or experience, attempt to marry revelation and reason. The debate that has continued through the centuries lives on as the problem of natural theology.

Neither side to the debate has given much attention to the dialogical character of Plato's method (except that, particularly in recent centuries, thought itself has been construed as having a dialogical or dialectical character). Whereas it is true that Platonism posits the innateness of truth, there is at least the suggestion in Plato that the truth that is innate is discovered not by introspection or by reflection but by dialogue.

The Platonic legacy, then, points us to a possibility that cannot be ignored in the contemporary context. Dialogue has been described as a way of sharing truth or as a way of communicating it. In these descriptions it is assumed that the truth that is communicated or shared is a truth that one or both parties to the dialogue already possess. The Platonic legacy points us to the possibility that dialogue may be a condition of truth, a way of knowing truth that is not possessed by any one of the dialogical partners alone. If this possibility is real, the truth to which dialogue leads may not be so completely opposed to revelation as the traditional debate has assumed.

MARTIN BUBER: I AND THOU

> We expect a theophany of which we know nothing but the place, and the place is called community. In the public catacombs of this expectation there is no single God's Word which can be clearly known and advocated, but the words delivered are clarified for us in our human situation of being turned to one another.[1]

That dialogue is a way to truth, indeed *the* way to truth, is an implication of the philosophy of Martin Buber. Buber speaks of dialogue in terms of the relationship of I and Thou. The terms themselves suggest a model of dialogue that is primarily a person-to-person encounter. Although it is true that the one-to-one relationship is the paradigm that Buber refers to most frequently, the reality to which Buber wishes to point by his use of the concept transcends the paradigm. Many of the things that Buber has to say about the I-Thou relationship illuminate the nature of dialogue between communities and between traditions. All dialogue is dialogue between people. There is much that can be learned about dialogue in general from the model of the person-to-person encounter.

Buber's philosophy has had considerable influence on the Christian theology of the twentieth century. On the whole, the point that Christian theologians have taken from Buber is that the I-Thou relationship is a model of the relationship between the individual and God. What Buber has had to say in a more general way about the nature of dialogue has not been so influential. It is Buber's understanding of dialogue, more than his understanding of God, that we need to take up here.

Buber distinguishes between two "attitudes," I-It and I-Thou. The word "attitude" is misleading. I-It and I-Thou are actually structures of reality. There is a structured reality that is named by the primary word "I-It." There is a structured reality that is named by the primary word "I-Thou." Without the structured reality we know as "I-It," we cannot survive. Without the structured reality we know as "I-Thou," our survival is empty, without meaning.

To understand Buber, we must appreciate that "I-It" and "I-Thou" are not compound words. They are primary words. To speak of a world to which the self relates, we must distinguish between "It" and "Thou." The world is an abstraction from one of the primary words. The world we know as "It" can never, therefore, be equated with the world we encounter as "Thou." The world exists in, and not apart from, one of these two attitudes. Similarly, there is no independent self that relates now to "It," now to "Thou." Like the world, the self is an abstraction from a primary word. The "I" of "I-It" cannot be equated with the "I" of "I-Thou."

The "I-It" and "I-Thou" can be distinguished by where, in the two structures, reality is centered. In "I-It," reality is centered in the self. "It" is the world as it is known, experienced, and used by a subject. When I experience the world, when I know the world, when I use the world, the cosmos is centered in me. I "own" my experience, my knowledge, my technology. Things are valued, and they receive their significance, in relation to me.

In the "I-Thou" relationship, I do not experience. I do not know. I am addressed. I encounter. In the spatial image of a center, the cosmos centers not in me, but in a point between I and Thou. The Thou, Buber says, "fills the heavens. This does not mean that nothing exists except himself. But all else lives in his light."[2]

The distinction between "It" and "Thou" is not the distinction between the human/nonhuman; nor is it the distinction between the animate/inanimate. The difference between "It" and "Thou" is not the difference between a person and a thing. One of Buber's prime examples of the difference between the "I-It" and the "I-Thou" is that of a tree. In the example, Buber cites a number of ways in which a tree can be studied or observed. It makes no difference if the observation is done with the eye of the scientist or that of the artist. As that which is observed, the tree is an "It." Buber continues:

It can, however, also come about, if I have both will and grace, that in considering the tree I become bound up in relation to it. The tree is now no longer It. I have been seized by the power of exclusiveness.[3]

A further example that is very important to Buber's understanding of the relationship between "I-Thou" and "I-It" is the story that Buber tells of his relationship as a young boy to a horse on his grandparents' estate:

I used, as often as I could do it unobserved, to steal into the stable and gently stroke the neck of my darling, a broad dapple-grey horse. It was not a casual delight but a great, certainly friendly, but also deeply stirring happening. If I am to explain it now, beginning from the still very fresh memory of my hand, I must say that what I experienced in touch with the animal was the Other, the immense otherness of the Other, which, however, did not remain strange like the otherness of the ox and the ram, but rather let me draw near and touch it. When I stroked the mighty mane, sometimes marvellously smooth-combed, at other times just as astonishingly wild, and felt the life beneath my hand, it was as though the element of vitality itself bordered on my skin, something that was not I, was certainly not akin to me, palpably the other, not just another, really the Other itself; and yet it let me approach, confided itself to me, placed itself elementally in the relation of Thou and Thou with me. . . . But once—I do not know what came over the child, at any rate it was childlike enough—it struck me about the stroking, what fun it gave me, and suddenly I became conscious of my hand. The game went on as before, but something had changed, it was no longer the same thing. And the next day, after giving him a rich feed, when I stroked my friend's head he did not raise his head. A few years later, when I thought back to the incident, I no longer supposed that the animal had noticed my defection. But at the time I considered myself judged.[4]

The examples of the tree and the horse, both drawn from the nonhuman world, underscore that for Buber the possibility of dialogue, which is the possibility of relation, is not dependent on a prior valuation of the other. Dialogue is not based on whether the Thou is intelligent enough or worthy enough to relate to me. In dialogue, there is no a priori decision that the other is qualified to speak to me and to be heard by me before dialogue can begin.

There is a feature of the example of the horse of which we need to take special attention. Buber expresses the "Thou-ness" of the horse in terms of the "other." The Thou is not I. It is precisely when Buber ceases to be caught up in the otherness of the horse that the relationship is destroyed. It is as Buber attends to his own reactions to the horse that dialogue ceases.

This depiction of the I-Thou as an encounter with otherness occurs and reoccurs throughout Buber's work. We need to note that this view is quite different from what we might describe as a common-sense view of dialogue. In the common sense view, dialogue is made possible, not by otherness, but by sameness. Common sense holds that dialogue is possible only when the parties to dialogue have "something in common." Buber's understanding of the I-Thou encounter does not require common ground as a precondition to dialogue. We will need to return to this point in later chapters.

REFLECTIONS ON PLATO AND BUBER

Both Plato and Buber raise the suggestion that dialogue is a means to truth. Dialogue is not understood by either as a way of sharing truth that one or both parties already have. Rather, it is a way of knowing truth that neither party possesses prior to the dialogue.

Here Buber goes further than Plato. In Plato, we actually have the truth potentially before dialogue. After dialogue we have knowledge of the truth as our own possession. Dialogue is the means of knowing truth, the way our potential knowledge is made actual. For Buber, however, truth is not primarily something we get out of the encounter. Truth is not a possession. It exists not in the I but between I and Thou. Truth is not a by-product of the encounter. Truth is the encounter.

Christian theology has always had difficulties with Platonic philosophy, even when Plato has been adopted as the primary philosophical resource for theology. We have already seen some of those difficulties. Buber's approach, on the other hand, raises difficulties of its own. These difficulties need to be named.

Buber's view of truth as relationship is closely connected with his doctrine of God. According to Buber, God is the "eternal Thou," "the Thou that by its very nature cannot become It."⁵ The eternal Thou, Buber holds, is encountered in every particular Thou. Consequently, for Buber, "there is no such thing as seeking God for there is nothing in which he could not be found."⁶

To recall our discussion of the theology of Karl Barth, Buber seems to be pointing to the I-Thou relationship as definitive of God. The I-Thou encounter would seem to be Buber's ultimate criterion that guides his understanding of the meaning of language about God. To identify God, Buber points to the I-Thou relationship.

Buber's location of the encounter of God in the encounter with others has much to commend it. It would allow Buber to account for the reality of God's presence in traditions outside his own. It makes sense of the universality of God's presence. Since God cannot become It, the reality of God in the other does not depend on any special content, any doctrine or idea that the other may hold. God, like truth, exists not in the I, not in the other, but between I and Thou.

There is little problem for the Christian in joining Buber in pointing to dialogue as a place where God is known. The problem for many (though not all) Christians arises when dialogue is made definitive of the encounter with God. How, we might ask, can Buber's account be reconciled to a Christian doctrine of the Incarnation?

That, we must hasten to admit, is not Buber's problem. Buber's answer is one that presents no problem to many Christians. As a Jew, Buber is able to speak unusually positively about Jesus. He can speak about Jesus even as a "son of God" in respect of the openness of Jesus to relationship. Yet in the last analysis, in Buber's approach God is "in Christ" in the same way and in the same sense as God is present in any other human being. For Buber, as for much Christian liberalism, the divinity of Christ is simply the realization of the capacity for divinity that is open to every human being.

Both Plato and Buber represent dialogue as a way to truth. Both support their view of dialogue with a theory that accounts for the power of dialogue to convey truth. Plato's theory of dialogue involves the postulation of an eternal world of universals which can be "recollected" by a dialogical method. Buber's theory rests on the identification of God as the eternal Thou who is encountered in every particular Thou.

Of these theories of dialogue, Buber's is likely to present fewer difficulties for the Christian believer. However, Buber's theory does not meet the concerns of those Christian traditions that have stressed "special revelation." To these traditions, the revelation of God in Jesus Christ is not simply one example among many of God's self-revelation in dialogue. Buber's theory would not seem to support those views that would acknowledge a definitive revelation by God in one particular event or person.

This, it should be noted, is not a uniquely Christian problem. Most Muslims would not be comfortable in seeing Allah's dictation of the Qur'an to Mohammed as simply one example among many of God's universal self-revelation in the I-Thou relationship. Buber's theory can stand as an account of God's activity in universal human experience. It creates problems if it is seen as a theology of revelation.

In many traditions, including the Christian tradition, truth has been considered to be a possession that has had to be defended against dialogue. Dialogue has been seen as a potential source of the corruption of truth. In this context, the suggestion that dialogue is a source of truth is crucial. How, we must ask, can the promise of dialogue as a way to truth be affirmed by criteria that are acceptable to particular religious traditions?

Some commentators on interfaith dialogue suggest that it is not possible. Particularist criteria of truth have to be given up in order for genuine dialogue to be possible. Thus, it is argued, Christians must recognize that the revelation of God in Jesus Christ is but an alternative form of the revelation of God as it is known in other traditions. For Christians to insist that the revelation of God in Jesus Christ is somehow definitive is to preempt the possibility of genuine interfaith dialogue.

There may, however, be a possible approach to dialogue that does not require religious believers to relativize that which in their faith is decisive. Is there a place in Christian theology for the affirmation that dialogue is a means for the discovery of truth? Is a theory of dialogue possible in Christian theology? Buber's theory is promising so long as it is seen as an account of God's continuing presence in the world. For many Christians, and others, it will not seem promising as a doctrine of revelation. The crucial question is whether a theology of dialogue requires such a universalistic doctrine of revelation. It is the argument of this book that it does not.

9

Preparation for Conversion

"Dialogue" is a word that is used in common speech with a variety of meanings. "Dialogue" can mean simply "chatting." It can refer to a very formal process of conversations at the official level between representatives of different groups. It can refer to a purely linguistic exchange between the dialogue partners. It can also mean an encounter that goes far beyond the merely verbal level. The loose way in which the word is used makes possible a wide variety of perspectives about what "dialogue" is and what it is for. We need to look at some of these perspectives.

The first perspective that we will examine has a long and distinguished history in Christendom. Since at least the second century, this has been the perspective of most Christians who wanted to promote positive relations with non-Christian communities and their traditions. Dialogue (although this word was not generally used) with other traditions was justified by the assertion that the other traditions were not outside God's saving and revealing care but that, in those traditions, God had laid a basis that would be fulfilled by the Gospel of Jesus Christ. Other traditions, in short, were preparations for the Gospel.

The claim that other traditions are preparation for the Gospel has not necessarily been made generally of all other traditions. When it has been used as an argument for a dialogical relation with another tradition, it may be claimed that the ignorance or hostility that characterizes most "unbelievers" is not true of the particular tradition with which dialogue is desired. While the claims of most other traditions can be discounted and disputed by Christian missionaries, the argument might run, this particular tradition is different. Its claims are compatible with at least some of the things that are believed by Christians.

This claim, that other traditions are preparation for the Gospel, has been made with differing results in the Christian tradition. At least implicitly, this was one of the earliest attitudes towards Judaism among Christians. Insofar as Christ was seen as the fulfillment of the law and the prophets, the law and the prophets were understood as preparatory to the Gospel event. The Hebrew scriptures, Christian apologetics has often claimed, speak of Christ. This theme has continued to reappear in Christian attitudes to Judaism, even though its affect has usually been muted by theologies of isolation and hostility.

The perspective that sees another tradition as a preparation for the Gospel has had its most profound effect on the Christian tradition in relation to philosophy. Some early theologians, of which the classical example is Justin Martyr, who lived and taught in the middle of the second century, argued that the greatest of the Greek philosophers, like Plato, were not to be treated by Christians as if they were ordinary pagans. The Logos which took flesh in Jesus Christ was the same as the Logos of which the Greek philosophers spoke. Plato, Justin Martyr argued, had read Moses and much of his teaching spoke the same truth that could be found in the Hebrew scriptures.

It may be necessary to remind ourselves here that, in the early years of Christian history, philosophy was not regarded as a secular academic discipline that was more or less neutral when it came to religious questions. Greek philosophy, in many respects, had developed as religion for the sophisticated elite. In the case of Parmenides, the religious dimension of philosophy had been quite explicit. Even so, the various other schools of Greek philosophy—Epicurianism, Stoicism, Platonism, and so on—were generally regarded and behaved as quasi religious movements. The case had to be made, therefore, that at least some of the philosophical schools should be treated differently by Christians than the other religious sects of the pagan world.

The current view that philosophy is a secular resource to Christian theology was by no means self-evident to the early Christians. The view that Justin Martyr advanced, that at least some of the Greek philosophers anticipated the truth that was fully revealed in Jesus Christ, was a first step toward the secularization of philosophy in Christian culture. At the very least, it implied that the methods of the philosophers were not incompatible with the truth of the Gospel. The definition of philosophy as a secular discipline allowed Christian theologians to draw on its resources without feeling that they were flirting with "strange gods." Justin Martyr's approach to philosophy was, in many respects, naïve and unsophisticated. It laid the basis, however, for the eventual incorporation of philosophy as a resource in the Christian theological curriculum.

Justin Martyr's approach to philosophy was not self-evident to the early Christians. Philosophy could be regarded by Christians, and was by some, as the "wisdom of this world" that was made valueless by the "foolishness of God" (I Corinthians 1:25). Tertullian, writing in the early third century, dismissed philosophy with the rhetorical question, "What has Athens to do with Jerusalem?" Tertullian's radical separation of Christ and culture implied that philosophy was at best an exercise in ignorance.

Justin Martyr's view of philosophy as preparatory to the Gospel, was given sophisticated expression in Augustine and in Aquinas. Augustine, who was actually hostile to most philosophical movements, nevertheless saw value in a purified Platonism. His view of the human soul, ruled by reason, as the seat of the image of God in human nature, allowed philosophy to be viewed as a "point of contact" with the Gospel. The exploration of the human mind with philosophical resources provided an appropriate analogy for the exposition of the fullness of divine truth as revealed in and by Jesus Christ.

The philosophy that was legitimized by Augustinian theology was Platonic. When Aristotelian philosophy began to make an impact in Europe, around the thirteenth century, Thomas Aquinas and others had to make the case that Aristotelian philosophy ought not to be regarded as incompatible with Christian faith. The case had to be made in the light of the fact that Aristotelian philosophy was already being used to support Islamic theology. In short, Aristotelian philosophy was suspect first, not only because it was at variance with the Platonic tradition in Christian thought, but also because of its association with Islam.

The victory that Aristotelianism achieved in and through the theology of Thomas Aquinas was made possible because Aquinas was able to interpret Aristotle as preparatory to the Gospel. What appears as naïve in Justin Martyr receives a profound and sophisticated expression in Aquinas. Aristotelian philosophy becomes the means whereby the knowledge of God which is natural to all people, and which is crowned and completed by the Gospel, can be intelligibly expressed and related to the truth of revelation.

The way in which Aquinas justified his use of Aristotle implied the existence of truth in all non-Christian religious traditions. Muslims, for example, could use Aristotle because Aristotelian philosophy represented the pinnacle of natural knowledge—knowledge that is available to all human beings by virtue of reason alone. Because all human beings are rational, all human beings have access to the natural rational knowledge that philosophers in general and Aristotle in particular expound. The natural knowledge that is available through reason needs, in Aquinas' theology, completion and fulfillment by revelation. It follows that all traditions, insofar as they are not totally irrational, may be seen as preparation for the full truth as it is known in sacred doctrine, the teachings of the Christian Church.

In the development of the relationship between philosophy and theology, we see something of the dynamic of the perspective that looks on other traditions as preparation for the Gospel. In the first place, to declare a movement, tradition, or idea as preparatory to the Gospel, rules out the options of seeing the movement, tradition or idea as superstitious or as hostile to the Gospel. Traditionally, then, the argument that a tradition is preparatory to the Gospel has been used to counter a prevailing theology of isolation or hostility towards the movement in question.

Secondly, the argument that a movement is preparatory to the Gospel has traditionally been used to support a dialogical approach to the movement in question. Theologians like Justin Martyr and Thomas Aquinas, who took this approach to philosophy, did so precisely because they wanted to open and/or continue a conversation between theology and philosophy. Conversely, theologians who have not been interested in a conversation with philosophy have been inclined to depict philosophy more as a movement that is intrinsically hostile to Christian faith.

The perspective that other movements are preparatory to and completed by Christian faith has only recently gone out of favor as a justification for dialogue. As recently as the early 1960s, Christians like Raimundo Pannikar and R. C. Zaehner were attempting to justify a dialogical relationship with Hinduism on this basis.

The perspective functions as justification for dialogue only when the prevailing view of another tradition is one of isolation or hostility. When the prevailing view is more open, the perspective that views other traditions as merely preparatory to the fullness of Christian faith is questioned for its triumphalist assumptions.

This would seem to have been the fate in recent years of this approach to dialogue. The suggestion that other traditions are intrinsically incomplete, that only Christians are in a position to know what another tradition really means, has not commended the approach to the more enthusiastic supporters of interfaith dialogue. Pannikar, in fact, abandoned this approach in his revision of *The Unknown Christ of Hinduism*. Karl Rahner's notion of "anonymous Christians" among other religious traditions has been criticized, perhaps unjustly, for suggesting the same approach.

Paradoxically, this perspective has now been adopted by some who are wary of interfaith dialogue or, perhaps more accurately, who are concerned that an emphasis on dialogue not destroy the evangelistic mission of the Church. The Lausanne Occasional Papers represent, as far as it can be represented in a single source, the most careful statement of an evangelical consensus of what the world mission of the Church is, and how that mission relates to other religious traditions. The non-Christian religions are often treated as legitimate human religious quests. The answers to those quests can ultimately be found not in those traditions but in Jesus Christ. The approach that is typically urged by the Lausanne papers is that the religious quest and its symbols as represented by other traditions be taken as the starting point. These non-Christian traditions—Islam, Buddhism, Hinduism—prepare their adherents for the Gospel by raising the right questions. The implication of this, for evangelicals, is that a dialogue with other traditions that helps us to understand the other is quite in order. The relationship, however, must not stop with dialogue. Christians, in encounter with non-Christian traditions, must go beyond dialogue and "proclaim Christ."

The perspective that sees other traditions as preparatory to the Gospel inevitably reflects or suggests a theology of competition. Truth is acknowledged as present in the other tradition, but the fullness of truth is to be found only in Christian faith. One can indeed be open to discovering new truth in this type of dialogue. In the last analysis, however, the truth we discover in traditions that are merely preparatory to our own is a truth that "we should have known all along." When compared to a theology of isolation or a theology of hostility, this perspective seems open, understanding, and inclusive. Outside the context of prevailing negative views of other traditions, however, the sense of superiority inherent in this perspective makes it appear arrogant and insensitive. The perspective that sees dialogue as a means of conversion must necessarily view the prospective dialogue partner as in need of conversion. The other tradition is consequently seen as lacking the fullness of truth that is present in our own. If we decide in advance who the others are and determine in advance how much truth the others are permitted to possess, we subvert in advance any potential dialogical relation. One or both parties enter the relationship in order to teach. Invariably they will not teach, but debate. The perspective is competitive, not dialogical, from the very start.

10

Dialogue as Negotiation

We have already seen how the ecumenical movement expressed the growth of an intra-Christian theology of partnership. As competitive relationships between churches became less appropriate to the context in which churches lived and worked, churches came more and more to view each other as more or less equivalent expressions of the same faith. Of course differences remained, but the differences came more and more to be perceived as nonessentials, items that were open to negotiation.

Because the differences between the churches in the ecumenical movement were seen as negotiable, negotiation became the point of the churches' conversations with each other. As the word "dialogue" came to be used of interchurch conversations, negotiation became a dominant paradigm in understanding dialogue. From the perspective of the ecumenical movement, dialogue appears as a form of negotiation.

Negotiation is an activity that involves two or more parties, the aim of which is agreement. It presupposes that the divergent interests of the parties may not have to preclude some form of common action. The differences between the parties are assumed to be, or are at least hoped to be, nonessential to the action contemplated. In order that agreement may be reached, it is assumed that one or both sides will have to make some concessions.

As a form of human interaction, negotiation is "at home" in business and political deals. At its best, negotiation is a highly skilled form of human interaction that attempts to have all parties leave the table feeling like winners. At its worst, negotiation is an attempt by one party to "beat the other down," to force compromises on the other party at every opportunity and with no loss to itself.

The suitability of negotiation to business and politics make it an essential ingredient in discussions for which the goal is church union. The divergent interests of complex institutions like churches need to be negotiated if the institutions wish to merge. That is exactly the type of situation that the negotiating process is for!

Short of organic union, negotiation is the appropriate process for religious groups engaged in joint action. Whether the joint action be an interfaith coalition on Peace and Development or a Week of Prayer service, the conditions of each church's participation in the common activity must be jointly discussed and agreed upon. Where agreement is the goal, negotiation is the process, and compromise the cost.

The relations between churches, however, are not just a matter of business and politics. The discussion between churches has involved conversation about faith as well as action.

The distinction here between faith and action is not clear cut. A confession of faith is, among other things, an action. When two churches are discussing a common confession or a common statement, they are attempting to perform a common action. In this situation, negotiation is the appropriate process for producing such a statement. Agreement is still the goal.

Because common statements have often been the goal of ecumenical conversations, dialogue has often appeared to be just another word for negotiation. Because compromise is part and parcel of the negotiation game, much of the literature on dialogue, particularly literature that has been informed by the ecumenical movement, has a distinctly cautious tone. "Syncretism" is the name that is given to the danger of compromise.

One often meets, in the literature on dialogue, the assumption explicitly stated that dialogue is the search for agreement. Even in dialogues concerning faith and belief that do not anticipate issuing common statements, it is stated that the dialogical method involves the search for "common ground." Without common ground, it is asserted, dialogue cannot proceed.

Stated that generally, it is difficult to argue with the assumption. To engage in dialogue, the parties must both be able to talk (i.e., they must share a common humanity) and they must want to talk. They must share a common desire. If that is what is meant by "common ground," it is certainly a precondition of dialogue. Yet one suspects that, when this term is used, something more specific is meant. It suggests that there are one or more "truths" of a spiritual nature, statements of faith, that are shared by both sides. From a starting point on what is held in common, the parties work at clarifying and, if possible, reconciling their differences.

The existence of common ground between differing Christian churches has not been hard to find. The differences between Christian communities have been important and serious. The divisions that these differences have caused have often been inevitable. Nevertheless, even among the most different Christian communities there are usually large areas of "common ground." These groups will usually attribute some authority to the Bible, and they will acknowledge Jesus Christ as, in some sense, the author and even object of Christian faith. They will usually, although not inevitably, acknowledge the sacraments of baptism and the eucharist. They will have, in many respects, common assumptions about the being of God and about human nature.

In the context of Christian ecumenism, then, the notion that dialogue is like negotiation has some basis in the fact that differing Christian groups share common sources and, to a considerable extent, a common history. It is not unnatural then for Christians in dialogue with each other to start with what is shared and to proceed from there to more divisive issues.

The negotiation model of dialogue also makes some sense when it is extended to dialogue between Christians and their nearest religious relations: Judaism and Islam. Both these traditions share with Christianity a commitment to monotheism as well as much of the mythology, legends, and history of ancient Israel. In this interfaith dialogue, the common ground may be more difficult to define and the divergences more apparent than in intra-Christian dialogue, but the negotiation model is still a plausible one.

The negotiation model is not very helpful when the parties to dialogue come from very different historical traditions and think in very different conceptual categories. In cases where the parties to dialogue are so different, it is not always possible to define any "common ground" as the starting point for dialogue. Even if some similarities can be identified between such divergent traditions, those similarities are understood in such different contexts that it is not always possible to have any clear sense in which both parties may be said to be talking about "the same thing." Similarly, the points at which the traditions seem most different have such differing contexts in the belief and practice of the traditions that it is not always possible to be confident that the traditions are contradicting each other.

Consider the case of the relationship between Christianity, as a Western monotheistic tradition, and Buddhism, an Eastern nontheistic tradition. Between Christianity and Buddhism some similarities can be found. Both traditions have a "founder," Jesus of Nazareth and Siddhartha Gottama respectively. Both traditions refer to their founder with a special title that indicates his spiritual significance, Christ and Buddha. Both traditions originated as reform movements in relation to their parent traditions: Judaism and Hinduism. In a very general sense, both traditions are concerned with the salvation of all humanity.

Yet even in these respects there is very little that could be used as common ground for dialogue. Jesus Christ and Gottama Buddha have very different significance in the respective traditions. Jesus Christ is considered by most Christians, at least in some sense, as a unique manifestation of God. Gottama Buddha is one enlightened being among many, the historical Buddha being significant only as the discoverer and propagator of the teaching (dharma) that makes enlightenment possible. Christianity understands salvation as the answer to human sin. Enlightenment, in Buddhism, is the answer to human suffering. It is therefore illusory to suggest that Buddhism and Christianity are both concerned with salvation. "Salvation" in the two traditions has very different connotations. Indeed to even call Buddhist enlightenment "salvation" is to run the danger of reading Christian expectations into Buddhist teaching.

A naïve Christian response to other religious traditions has tended to make certain assumptions that, as we have become more knowledgeable and sophisticated, have proved very hard to break. One of the most persistent of these assumptions is that religion is about the gods. Consequently the question that has had to be asked in establishing common ground with another tradition is whether it worshipped "the same God" as that who is worshipped by Christians. John Hick argues for his "Copernican" view of other religions by arguing that all major traditions worship the same God. Scholars as diverse as Stanley Samartha, Paul Knitter, and Alan Rice urge a theocentric rather than a Jesucentric Christology on the grounds that God is the common denominator of religious traditions.

We have already seen that a theology of partnership has difficulty with the question of idolatry. What is an idol, and how would you know that somebody was worshipping one? There is another problem, however, with a theology that portrays dialogue as a kind of negotiation based on a common worship of the same God by all traditions.

Judaism, Christianity, and Islam are theocentric traditions. The identity of God and the worship of the one so identified, are central to these traditions. Christians have tended to assume that this theocentricism is common to all religions.

There are traditions, however, that are nontheistic. Buddhism is the most notable example of a nontheistic tradition. It is not that Buddhism is officially atheistic, but rather that it regards the question of the existence of God and the gods as irrelevant to the quest for enlightenment. Whether one believes in a God or does not so believe makes no difference to what Buddhists would understand as "salvation." Buddhism has been included in theocentric arguments for dialogue only through a distortion of Buddhism into a form of theism or by an appeal to one particular sect of Buddhism (e.g., Pure Land) where faith in a savior figure has some of the appearance of Western theism.

The centrality of God clearly does not provide us with common ground for a negotiating type of dialogue with nontheistic traditions. But it is also questionable whether theocentricism provides common ground with traditions that include belief in and worship of beings that are analogous to the gods of the Western traditions. From the fact that a religious tradition includes belief in God or gods, it does not follow that the belief in and worship of God is central to the tradition.

In Hinduism, for example, one finds many gods. Not all the gods of Hinduism are worshipped by and believed in by all Hindus. The Hindu tradition encompasses a rich polytheism, a philosophical monotheism, a practical atheism, and much more beside. One can believe in one God, believe in many gods, or not believe in any God and still be a faithful practicing Hindu.

One cannot assume a priori that the centrality of God can be taken as "common ground" in a dialogue with Hinduism. Some Hindus might be comfortable with this suggestion. Others might find it quite unacceptable. A plausible case can be made that if there is any center to Hinduism, it is more like the focus of Buddhism in the liberation of the self from the wheel of rebirth and the law of karma rather than in the belief in and worship of God or gods. The assumption of Western monotheism that religion is centered in the worship of God cannot be imposed a priori as the starting point of the dialogue.

A similar problem arises in a slightly different way in relation to Shinto and many of the so-called Primal religions of the world. Shinto believes in the existence of spiritual beings called "kami" (a word sometimes translated as "gods"). The kami, like the spirits of Primal traditions, have not been given any standard metaphysical definition. They appear as nature spirits, as the spirits of departed ancestors, and as the gods of the traditional mythology. The distinction between these spirits may not be clearly defined. In relation to Shinto and the Primal traditions, it cannot be assumed that their "spirits" are translatable into what the monotheistic traditions mean by God.

If negotiation, that is, the search for agreement, may seem an appropriate model for dialogue between the monotheistic traditions, it is more problematical when applied as a model of dialogue between a monotheistic tradition and a tradition of another type. In addition to the problem of locating the common ground that the dialogue will presuppose, the negotiating model of dialogue is vulnerable, within Christian circles at least, to the charge of syncretism.

North Atlantic theology in the twentieth century has been very sensitive to the danger of syncretism. My own experience may be typical of my generation of theologians who were trained in "main line" Protestant theological schools. I was introduced to the word "syncretism" very early in my theological training. The way the word was used left no doubt in anybody's mind that syncretism was *not* a good thing. One was left with the impression that there was a pure Gospel that was expressible in Hebrew thought forms. The history of the Church in attempting to translate that Gospel into the thought forms of other cultures was on the whole a not very happy one. The Gnostic movement of the second century and the liberal movement of the nineteenth century were probably the worst culprits when it came to syncretism.

A full explanation of the fear of syncretism in modern theology would be very complex. Two factors probably deserve special mention. The first factor was the reaction to liberalism among young European theologians after World War I. This reaction is most commonly associated with the name of Karl Barth but includes all of the so-called "dialectical theologians" of the 1920s—Bultmann, Brunner and Gogarten—and, somewhat less obviously, it might also be seen as including Paul Tillich. The cosy synthesis of religion and culture that had marked European theological liberalism was opposed in dialectical theology by a God who stood over against our culture and our idea making. God was portrayed as judge as well as creator and preserver. The accommodation of theology to bourgeois ideology was seen, in the last analysis, as infidelity to the Gospel.

A second factor in the concern about syncretism in twentieth-century theology was the experience of the Church in Europe under the Nazi regime. Christians in Northern Europe were faced in Nazism with a particularly pernicious revival of paganism. The Church learned how seductive this revived paganism was and how easy accommodation to the ideology of Nazism led to complicity in a demonic system. This may partially explain why, in the World Council of Churches, it is the Northern Europeans, who have little direct contact with Hindus, Buddhists, and Muslims, who are most nervous about the potential for syncretism in the dialogue with other faiths.

Visser t'Hooft, then General Secretary of the World Council of Churches, published in the early 1960s a study of syncretism entitled *No Other Name*.[1] By syncretism, Visser t'Hooft meant any attempt to create a common religion by bringing together features of all the major religions of the world. To prevent that danger, he argues against any syncretism that would compromise the Churches' commitment to the unique activity of God in Jesus Christ.

Whatever the pros and cons of the establishment of a religion that includes all religions, it is difficult to see syncretism as a danger to dialogue unless the goal of dialogue is construed as achieving agreement. The danger of syncretism as it is described by Visser t'Hooft arises when two parties reduce their claims to the lowest common denominator, precisely for the purpose of reaching agreement. When syncretism is feared as a result of dialogue, the presupposition that dialogue is a form of negotiation is lurking somewhere in the background.

Dialogue, understood as the search for agreement, has been important in the birth and growth of the Christian ecumenical movement. The achievements of this type of dialogue need to be acknowledged and appreciated. The search for agreement is not, however, constitutive of dialogue. If agreement is the goal of dialogue, and therefore the test of its value, many possible dialogical relationships will not be tried and, if they are tried, will prove to be exercises in frustration.

Rather than defining dialogue as a search for *agreement*, it would be more helpful to define dialogue as a search for *understanding*. To understand another tradition, I do not have to agree with its precepts. I do not have to create "common ground" in order to proceed. I may come to agree. I may find common ground. Insofar as that happens, it will be a gift of grace, an added bonus. In a dialogue I will seek to understand and to allow myself to be understood. If there is a threat of syncretism in the search for understanding, then to avoid syncretism I would have to close myself to reality, to confirm the integrity of my faith in splendid isolation from all of life.

Dialogue between divergent traditions, like Christianity and Buddhism, will be enhanced if understanding rather than agreement is the primary goal of dialogue. Whereas it is difficult, with traditions that speak in differing "languages," to speak of "common ground," it is not difficult in the contemporary world to speak of a mutual need to understand. We come to understand, not by reading about each other but in encountering each other, by hearing each other's language actually being spoken.

Yet even among Christians, it is doubtful that the search for agreement should continue to be considered as the primary goal of dialogue. The negotiation model of dialogue is strongly influenced by the example of official conversations between denominational authorities. It is at that level that the negotiating model is most appropriate. But the concept of dialogue needs to include groups of lay people whose primary need is to understand how their neighbors see the world as much as it includes denominational executives in charge of interfaith relations.

Even at the official level, agreement may not be the goal of interdenominational dialogue. A case in point is the official dialogue between the United Church of Canada and the Canadian Council of Catholic Bishops. This dialogue, authorized by the two churches in 1974, does not have the production of shared statements or of draft agreements between the churches as one of its goals. The United Church is not representative of a single confessional tradition and the dialogue cannot simply do on a national level what confessional bilaterals do at the international level. The dialogue is a conversation between a national church and the national council of bishops of an international communion. Goals that are often high on the agenda of interdenominational conversations—church union, mutual recognition of ministries, a common eucharist—are not on the immediate agenda but await developments at the international level.

The result has been that this dialogue, although officially sanctioned by the two churches, has not followed the negotiating model. It has attempted to explore areas of faith and morals, primarily to deepen appreciation of what it means to be Roman Catholic or United Church, what it is like to live in the other's universe of faith. The dialogue has focused on doctrine, on spirituality, on grass-roots concerns. It has not tried to formulate agreement. In fact, one of its better experiences of dialogue has been on an issue—abortion—where the group expected that no agreement would be possible. Common ground has been discovered rather than achieved.

The purpose of dialogue is understanding rather than agreement. That is not all dialogue is. Understanding comes first. It is the primary goal of dialogue. To what follows from this primary goal we now turn.

11

Dialogue as Integration

One of the claims that is often made for dialogue is that encounter with a different tradition does not make us less loyal to our own traditions. On the contrary, it is claimed, dialogue with another tradition leads us to a deeper understanding of and loyalty to our own faith traditions.

That claim, which I believe to be true, can probably only be validated by a personal experience of dialogue. It is not universally valid. Through dialogue, some people come to accept the position of their dialogue partner and experience conversion. Others do attempt a kind of syncretism, fashioning a very idiosyncratic kind of personal faith that does not quite belong to any tradition. Those kinds of results, which are feared by those who are concerned about the question of faithfulness in dialogue, are not the inevitable results of dialogue. Dialogue needs to be understood as holding promise rather than threat for faith.

Every religious tradition has its strong points and its weak points. Strength in one area is usually purchased at the cost of weakness in another area. Almost every Christian tradition would hold, for example, that personal piety needs to be balanced by a commitment to social responsibility. The balance is rarely achieved, however. A community that strongly emphasizes one ends up by giving little more than lip service to the other.

Dialogue allows one to gain perspective on the weak points of one's own faith by leading one to reflect on the strengths of others. In Christian dialogue, Catholics have been helped by the Protestant emphasis on scripture and preaching while Protestants have gained self-understanding by reflecting on Catholic eucharistic piety. In this dialogue, Protestants have not ceased being Protestant; nor have Catholics ceased being Catholic. Yet both have found the strength of the other to be a source of renewal for themselves.

I grew up in a predominantly Protestant community which was located in a predominantly Catholic area. In retrospect, I realize that we defined our Protestantism over against our stereotypes of the Catholicism of our neighbors. Catholicism was something foreign. It was superstitious, ritualistic, subservient to authority—everything that Protestantism was not.

As an undergraduate I would pass on my way from my home to classes a large grey stone building surrounded by a high stone wall. It was the Grand Seminaire, the seminary for the training of priests for the archdiocese of Montreal. On the green between the building and the stone wall, a statue of Mary could be glimpsed by the passerby through the open gate.

The world I would glimpse from time to time as I passed that gate was strange, foreign, and "other." I was only beginning to learn the words to describe it: *Tridentine, ultramontane.* It was the world of the Rosary, the Sacred Heart, devotion to saints, indulgences. It was everything that I was not.

Not many years later, I became involved in dialogue with Roman Catholics. Since then I have changed and so has Roman Catholicism.

I was led to reflect on my memories when, as a member of the bilateral discussion between my church and the Canadian Roman Catholics, I found myself staying in that grey stone building and looking out at the statue of Mary and the high stone wall, this time from the other side. The interior of the building is still Tridentine and ultramontane in its style. Yet I experience this world not as strange and foreign, but as a part of myself. Staying in that building is, for me, like visiting a relative. The furniture of that world is not mine. It reflects neither my beliefs, my tastes, nor my story. But it is nevertheless part of my world. It reflects stories that have been shared with me by people I have come to regard as part of my family.

I would use the word "integration" to describe what has happened to me since the thawing of Protestant-Catholic relations in the early 1960s. The reality of Catholic faith, Catholic piety, and Catholic tradition has become a part of my own heritage. I no longer define myself as a Protestant over against Catholicism. The four hundred years of Catholic history since the Reformation has once again become available to me as a Protestant Christian. I can look for spiritual renewal by retreating in a Trappist monastery as well as by seeking out "sound Biblical preaching." I can look for theological stimulation from Karl Rahner as well as from Karl Barth. I can hear and respond to the Word of God in Catholic and Protestant liturgy alike.

In the last chapter, I suggested that it is better to formulate the goal of dialogue as understanding than as agreement. Yet if we think of understanding as something that happens in our heads and something that is confined to our heads, then understanding is not adequate to express the goal of dialogue. The word "integration" is intended to point to the fact that genuine understanding has implications for our life and practice. Integration is something that happens "in our guts." In dialogue, more than just our theory is transformed.

We have already noticed at a number of points that the relation between philosophy and Christian faith has displayed many of the features of the relation between religious traditions. Philosophy, we have noted, has been variously represented by Christians as false knowledge, as intellectual rebellion against God, as less than fully adequate, and as a partner to religion in the search for truth.

It is worth considering, in this context, the way that Paul Tillich construed the relationship between philosophy and theology.[1] Tillich neither subjugates philosophy to theology, nor does he treat philosophy as a separate but equal road to truth. In Tillich theology and philosophy retain their own integrity. Nevertheless theology cannot isolate itself from philosophy. The dialogue with philosophy is not optional.

In Tillich's view of the relationship, both theology and philosophy deal with the same "object": being-itself. Philosophy is the rational inquiry into the structure of being. Theology is the systematic expression of ultimate concern for the God who is being-itself.

The conclusion that Tillich draws from his analysis is that there can be no agreement nor any contradiction between philosophy and theology. There can be agreement or conflict between philosophers and theologians, but only insofar as the theologian speaks as a philosopher or the philosopher speaks as a theologian.

We can understand Tillich as advocating an integration rather than a synthesis of philosophy and theology. The expression of ultimate concern (the theological task) needs to be informed by the best reflection available on the structure of being (the philosophical task).

Tillich's construal of the relationship of philosophy and theology is somewhat reminiscent of the Wittgensteinian notion of "language games."[2] In Wittgenstein, the concept of language games is introduced in protest against the idea, current in analytic philosophy, that all language could be reduced to a basic common language descriptive of objects in the world. Against this philosophical reductionism, Wittgenstein argues that languages arise out of and derive their meaning from their role in life, from activity. The meaning of words cannot be deduced a priori. The meaning of words needs to be understood from their role in life, from the "language games" in which they are used.

In Wittgensteinian terms, Tillich can be understood as suggesting that philosophy and theology are two distinct but related language games. The theologian needs to be bilingual, to have a working understanding of the language game of philosophy. Theology is informed by the other language game, but there is no third language to which theology and philosophy may be reduced.

There has been considerable disagreement among philosophers of religion concerning the application to religion of Wittgenstein's notion of language games. Those disagreements have concerned the question of the verification of language, the question of whether language about God could be evaluated in terms of descriptive language about the world, or whether language about God was a distinct and autonomous language game.

The verification question need not detain us here. A stronger case can be made that the idea of language games is more appropriately applied to the relation of religious traditions to each other. Might we think of the different religious traditions as distinct language games, exhibiting a complex web of similarities with and differences from each other, but ultimately not reducible to the language of the other?

When Christians approach other religious traditions, they have been inclined to ask questions like "Do these people worship the true God?" and "Does this religion lead people to salvation?" These questions, we might say, are a part of the Christian language game. In applying categories like "worship of the true God" and "salvation" to other religious traditions, we assume that these categories are applicable, that the members of the other tradition are playing the same "language game." At the very least, we assume that there is a universal religious language game of which Buddhism, Shinto, and Islam are each particular expressions. It further assumes that the universal religious language game looks very much like Christianity.

The concept of enlightenment in Buddhism is often taken as a variant of the Christian idea of salvation. The two concepts, however, derive their meaning from very different thought worlds. Enlightenment is a state of freedom from the attachments of ego. It is liberation from karma, from the wheel of rebirth. These are concepts that have no place in Judaeo-Christian thinking about salvation. In Christianity, salvation is liberation from alienation. Salvation is the restoration of the broken relationships between God, humanity, and the world. Clearly, Christian salvation and Buddhist enlightenment have important parallels. They have a functional similarity when the two traditions are compared. To treat them as the same concept, however, is to ignore the very different language games from which they derive their meaning. They may indeed commonly denote the ultimate human experience of liberation. The connotations of the concepts, however, are very different.

If religious traditions are more like distinct language games than they are like different dialects of the same language, then our understanding of the nature of dialogue will be quite different than it is if we were to use the negotiating model. If different religious traditions are but different dialects of a common language, then dialogue is the process by which we agree on the grammatical standards for the religious language. If, however, different religions are like different languages, then dialogue is more like the process by which one becomes bilingual.

Bilingualism is a useful analogy to what is meant here by integration. When one becomes bilingual, one learns to operate within the categories that are appropriate to each particular language. Each language is considered to have its own integrity. A category of one is not applied to the other, or, if it is, it is soon recognized as a mistake. Furthermore, the bilingual person does not usually have equal facility in both languages. One of the languages remains the "mother tongue" of the bilingual individual. At the same time, one comes to understand one's own language in a more profound way by experiencing it in contrast to a second language.

All of these things are true, in an analogous way, of dialogue. To enter into dialogue with another religious tradition is to come to see the world through other eyes. One comes to understand what their categories are, how they relate to each other, how they relate to the world. One even becomes able to anticipate how a member of another tradition will respond in certain circumstances. One begins to be able to use the concepts and categories of the other tradition for oneself. Most significantly, one is able to look at one's own faith and its categories through the eyes of the other. When that happens, we see things about ourselves and our faith that we had not seen before. In all of that, we do not cease to be committed and faithful members of our own tradition. We are on the way to becoming religiously bilingual.

12

Dialogue as Activity

Dialogue is often understood to be an event or an activity. It is one of the things among other things that people may (or may not) do. It is an endeavor that must be given a priority that is relative to all the other events and activities that fill our common life; each in turn has its own relative priority in our lives. In this sense, dialogue is an activity among other activities.

Interfaith dialogue, as an activity, is an occasion when representatives of different faiths assemble, formally or informally, to talk, to converse. Dialogues may be conversations about a wide range of things. The representatives of different traditions may be speaking out of common concern for a social issue. (Human rights is a common focus for interfaith conversation.) They may meet to debate a matter on which they disagree. They may converse in order to negotiate something that is important to their respective communities. They may converse in order that they might understand each other more adequately. They may meet with the object of converting each other. There is a wide range of topics that can qualify as appropriate subject matter for interfaith conversation.

Apart from the most xenophobic members of each tradition and apart from those cases where other traditions are interpreted by a theology of hostility, there is really no objection to dialogue within any religious community. Evangelicals, for example, may well insist that the relation has to go beyond conversation into evangelization, but there is no objection there to conversation as such. They may be concerned about accepting rules for conversation that would rule out the proclamation of the Gospel. But that is not an objection to conversation, to talking with people of other traditions. What concerns them is that nonevangelicals might set the rules for the conversation in such a way that the evangelical agenda is compromised and their position in the conversation made untenable.

If dialogue is an event or an activity that can include a wide variety of topics, the problem with interfaith dialogue is not whether it is a legitimate activity for a committed believer. The legitimacy of interfaith conversation will be widely granted by most religious communities. The main problem that needs to be addressed around the question of interfaith dialogue as an activity or event is the question of priority. Among all the pressing items on the agenda of any religious community, how important is it to hold conversations with people of other religious traditions? And of all the many different religious communities around us, whom should we speak to, given that we don't have the time and energy to organize dialogues with them all?

The question of the priority of interfaith dialogue is not as simple a question as may first appear. As long as interfaith dialogue is understood as those occasions when religious people of differing traditions gather to compare beliefs and practices, one suspects that interfaith dialogue will not be very high on the agenda of religious communities. In this sense, dialogue appears as a "motherhood" issue, one about which few disagree but which has very little to do with the more pressing matters of faith and life that preoccupy every religious community.

This appears to be a major factor in the failure of the World Council of Churches to give much more than token support to its program unit on Dialogue with People of Other Faiths and Ideologies. At the 1983 Assembly of the World Council of Churches, representatives of other religious traditions were present in greater numbers and were given a prominence that they had not enjoyed at any previous Assembly. When it came to doing business, however, the crunch issues of the Assembly revolved around peace and justice issues. The result was that the report on Program Guidelines, which more than any other document sets the priorities for the World Council between Assemblies (held approximately every seven years), made only passing reference to the Dialogue with People of Other Faiths and Ideologies and left the program unit without any clear mandate. The statement on dialogue with people of other faiths, a rather weak document, was never formally adopted by the Assembly but was left for the Central Committee to approve after the close of the Assembly. One is left with the impression that although the World Council believes that conversation with other religious traditions is a worthy activity, in the face of the pressing issues of the nuclear threat and the oppression of the poor throughout the world, interfaith dialogue must rank rather low on the ecumenical agenda.

With the urgency of the issues raised by the threat of the powers of death in the contemporary world, this may well seem to be a sane and appropriate statement of what the priorities of Christians have to be. It may be worthwhile, however, to set that perception alongside something else that happened locally during the Vancouver Assembly.

A few weeks before the opening of the Assembly in July 1983, the government of the Province of British Columbia introduced a "legislative package" that, among other things, removed the right of civil servants to bargain collectively, threatened programs designed for the poor and the handicapped, abolished the office responsible for the enforcement of human rights, and indicated that certain types of complaints about human rights violations would henceforth be treated as "trivial."

The opening of the Vancouver Assembly provided an unusual opportunity for concerned Christians in British Columbia to meet each other during the summer, to consult and to respond to the government's program. As a result, a statement was drafted ecumenically to be read at a protest rally in a nearby city. A few days later, a major rally was organized for Vancouver itself. In preparation for that rally, it became clear that the other religious communities in Vancouver were equally as concerned, if not more so because of their minority status, with the threat to human rights that seemed inherent to the government program. The result was that the original Christian statement, drafted by a group of local visitors to the Vancouver Assembly, became, with a little editing, an interfaith statement that was read to the rally by the chairperson of the local interfaith council, a Muslim.

These events undoubtedly were unnoticed by all but a few of the Canadians at the Assembly. Nevertheless, the incident represents an important fact about dialogue and about peace and justice issues in today's world. The fact is that the Christian Church is not the only religious community that is concerned with the nuclear threat and with the plight of oppressed peoples. Any appropriate response to the threat of the powers of death in the contemporary world must surely be made in concert with Jews, Muslims, Buddhists, Hindus—with concerned people of any and every religious tradition. In short, dialogue must be understood not as a recreation in which we can indulge when the real business has been done, but as a dimension that is integral to the "real business" itself. Action for peace and justice, done in full consciousness of the realities of the contemporary world, cannot but include interfaith dialogue as one of its dimensions.

Dialogue as an activity in which religious people may or may not engage, and the resultant question of the priority which that activity deserves, is an important concern for John Cobb in his book *Beyond Dialogue*. The title of the work itself reflects that concern. Dialogue, for Cobb, is basically a conversation in which people from one tradition talk to people from another tradition. The central thesis of the book, which focuses on dialogue between Christians and Buddhists, is that the relationship that begins in dialogue must move "beyond dialogue" and result in a mutual transformation of the two traditions.

In making his case, Cobb criticizes the World Council of Churches for its reluctance to give interfaith dialogue anything more than ambiguous and token support. This failure, Cobb suggests, is due to the espousal of the World Council of a secular theology that Cobb sees as rooted in Barth's treatment of religion as a human activity alongside other human activities. The result is that, in the scale of human activities to which the World Council attends, religion does not rank very high.

Curiously, however, Cobb does not proceed to make the claim, not altogether unknown in religious liberalism, that religion is a special activity that is of particular concern to the Christian Church. His response is more cautious and conservative. Cobb claims that certain traditions, in particular Buddhism, are in touch with a truth that Christians need to hear. The need, according to

Cobb, is mutual. As Christians need to listen to the truth that Buddhists perceive, so Buddhists need to listen to the truth that Christians perceive. In listening to and in responding to truth, Cobb claims, we will be led toward mutual transformation.

In Cobb's view, then, the question of priority is resolved by a judgment about the relation of the other tradition to truth. The major religious traditions of the world, Cobb would certainly argue, are in touch with a truth that we need to hear. Nevertheless there are groups whose contact with truth is dubious and with whom dialogue is not appropriate.

> Dialogue is not the appropriate relation to all alien movements. It is grounded in basic respect, in the recognition of wisdom and integrity. There are movements such as Nazism and the Ku Klux Klan in which Christians do not recognize the requisite wisdom and integrity. There are many movements about which we are uncertain. But the time is past when sensitive Christians can question the presence in our world of many alien movements which rightly claim our respect and from which we have something to learn. It is in relation to these that dialogue is appropriate.[1]

The phrasing of this statement is somewhat unfortunate since it implies that the Christian is somehow in a position to make a priori judgments about the truth and integrity of other traditions. Nevertheless, as a statement of how Christians might set priorities for dialogue, it is not unreasonable. If there is a choice between dialogue with Buddhists and dialogue with Nazis, there would not seem to be much contest. Dialogue with Buddhists would appear to have more promise. Yet we must note that, at least at this one point, Cobb's logic is not very different from the logic of a theology of isolation, the traditional missionary view. There are certain traditions with which we do not have dialogue because those traditions have nothing to teach us. What is disturbing is not the particular groups whom Cobb cites, but the absence of clear criteria for knowing that a group has "nothing to teach" us.

Related to this is the question of the relation of traditions to truth. Cobb's argument proceeds as if truth is something that is possessed, in different aspects and expressed in different ways, by some traditions but not by others. He makes it appear that the decision about the priority of dialogue depends on the quantity of truth another tradition possesses. Only those traditions who "have truth" which they can then teach to us are worth taking as dialogue partners.

The model of truth as something that is possessed is not a particularly helpful one, though it may be an old and familiar model. For centuries Christian rhetoric has taken truth to be something that is possessed. The possessors of truth have been the Catholic magesterium, converted evangelicals, the Reformed confessions, or simply "Christianity." Truth, in short, was something that we "had" that others did not "have."

It is difficult to see how this view of truth could issue in dialogue at all. If there is an economy of truth in which each tradition "possesses" a piece of it, conversation between two traditions would not be dialogue but alternating monologues. In a Christian-Buddhist dialogue, one would expect the Buddhists to teach the truth they "possessed" while the Christians listened and learned. From time to time the roles would reverse, the Christians becoming the teachers and the Buddhists the learners.

I would not for a moment suggest that this two-way lecture is what Cobb has in mind when he advocates dialogue between Christians and Buddhists. The problem is that the language Cobb uses to deal with the truth question seems to adopt that view of truth and leads us to expect that a calculus of truth will help us to set priorities in the realm of dialogue.

We might recall here the suggestion we found in Plato and Buber, that dialogue is not so much a process of sharing truth as it is of discovering it. That is to say, that it is probably true that a Buddhist with whom I converse may well teach me something that I did not previously know. I would certainly expect to learn something about Buddhism. I might well learn something about Japan or Tibet or Sri Lanka that would be new to me. But that exchange of information is not the ultimate point of the dialogue. The most significant way in which truth is discovered in dialogue is when I and my dialogue partner together discover something neither of us had known before.

The idea of truth as a possession is too problematical to be helpful here. If we use different terms, however, the point that Cobb is stating begins to make some sense to the question of priorities in dialogue. In place of economic models of truth, psychological categories might be less misleading.

The groups that Cobb cites with whom dialogue is not appropriate, the Nazis and the Ku Klux Klan, are both groups whose behavior can be described in terms of psychological pathology. For a start, both groups are paranoiac. A case could be further made that both groups are psychotic, out of touch with reality.

The relevance of psychological categories is that they remind us of the fact that there are some individuals and groups who are not capable of dialogue. This is not because we, from the perspective of our morally superior insight, categorize prospective dialogue partners into "good guys" and "bad guys." Rather it is because certain groups and individuals behave in a way that continually subverts the dialogical process. The problem is not that we could have dialogue with these groups but choose not to. The problem is that dialogue itself is impossible. We might choose to converse with the Ku Klux Klan, for example. Our conversation would not be dialogue. At best it would be long-term therapy which, if one were to be very optimistic, might one day become dialogue. Dialogue remains a legitimate choice with groups who do not exhibit pathological behavior and for whom we can grant are genuinely in touch with reality.

This last point would seem to suggest that not all conversations are dialogue. Without attempting to draw any fine lines around a definition of dialogue as an activity, we need to grant that some conversations are more dialogical than others. What we mean by this will become more apparent when we consider dialogue as a relationship in the next chapter.

There are all kinds of conversations. In some conversations, the search for mutual understanding may not be present at all. However, there may be at least an element of dialogue in conversations that are, on the surface, antagonistic and adversarial. Debate may not be dialogue. It does not follow that there is nothing dialogical to debates. Dialogue (involving openness, listening, mutual growth) may be present in any conversation.

Interfaith dialogue may have happened in the conversation between the Dalai Lama and Thomas Merton. It also may happen in a casual conversation between a Baptist and a Sikh over the back fence. By conversing, we learn to dialogue. Our first attempts to converse with strangers may be stumbling and inept. We may unwittingly do many things that subvert the dialogical process. When we look back, we may be very embarrassed by the memory of our arrogance, our ignorance, our naïveté. As an activity, dialogue is learned by practice. As we develop the skill of listening, the importance of dialogue and its priority among our various activities becomes clearer. We come to see dialogue not so much as an activity among other activities but as a quality that needs to pervade all our conversations and all our relationships.

13

The Dialogical Imperative

Dialogue as Relationship

It is often difficult, in discussion about dialogue, to distinguish between dialogue as an activity and dialogue as a relationship. If dialogue can happen only when people meet in openness and honesty, then it would seem that it is the *relationship* of honesty and openness more than the *activity* of conversation, that is constitutive of dialogue.

In this chapter we want to look at the dialogical relationship. We need to start by placing dialogue alongside the other relationships that can exist between communities: isolation, hostility, competition, and partnership. Alongside these types of relationships, dialogue presents us with another and, we will argue, preferable model for the way in which religious communities relate to each other.

What is a dialogical relationship? It may be helpful, in attempting to define it, to start with what a dialogical relationship is not.

To begin with the obvious, dialogue is not monologue. We may describe monologue as a relationship in which the attitudes and beliefs of one party are in no way affected by a second party. The agenda of the first party cannot be challenged by the second party. The first knows what he/she intends to say to the other. That agenda does not change as a result of how the second party responds to it.

Lectures, sermons, and public addresses are examples of monological activities. In the case of lectures, at least, the monologue may occasionally be interrupted by dialogue, but even here the interruption is temporary. Eventually the speaker returns to the topic, the agenda of the lecture.

In all of these monological activities one party, the speaker, has control of the agenda. Briefly, the speaker decides what has to be said and then says it. The listener listens. Knowledge or ideas are conveyed *from* the speaker *to* the listener. The speaker hopes to be understood. The listener hopes to understand. The relationship is not reciprocal.

The relationship types that we described earlier—isolation, hostility, competition, and partnership—are all monological insofar as the content of the relationships are determined a priori. A relationship of isolation is monological because it has been determined a priori that the other has nothing significant to say to us. A relationship of hostility discounts a priori anything that the other might say. Even things that sound good and true are, because of their source, discounted as one more piece of deception that is part of the other's conspiracy against God.

The relationships of competition and partnership are not as unambiguously monological as are those of isolation and hostility. Both are open, in principle, to the fact that the other may have something to offer, something worth listening to. Yet, in the last analysis, the relations remain monological. In competition, the other is heard only because a good competitor needs to know the competition. Consequently, the other is heard primarily so that the position of the competitor can be "answered." The agenda of selling our own product is never compromised in the face of anything the other has to say.

Of the four types of relationships, partnership is the one that is most open to dialogue. Yet even here the openness is qualified. One establishes the relationship on the basis of some predefined "common ground." As long as both parties are comfortable with the way "common ground" has been defined, and as long as the question of how that "common ground" is to be interpreted is not raised, a reasonably open dialogue is possible. But in a partnership relationship, everything that the other has to say is interpreted in the context of the common ground as understood by the hearer. In other words, nothing that the other says ever calls into question the agenda that is set by the "common ground."

This is something of a problem, for example, with Christians who attempt to argue for a theocentric approach to other religions. It is argued that belief in an ultimate universal creative Spirit is common to all religious traditions. We all worship "the same God," albeit by different names. As we have already noted, this assumption does not quite fit when an avowedly theistic tradition like Christianity encounters a nontheistic tradition like Buddhism. The Christian response in this situation is to attempt to find a quasi-deity, a "God by another name" in Buddhist Dharma.

The problem with that approach is that it does not listen to Buddhism seriously at the point that Buddhism claims to be nontheistic. Christians want to persist in finding a quasi-deity in Buddhism, either for the sake of the partnership or, on the other side, of convicting Buddhists of idolatry. When this happens, we can listen to Buddhists only insofar as what they say fits our theistic presupposition. To sacrifice the presupposition is to risk the very basis of the relationship.

On the Buddhist side, the practice of meditation has been proposed as "common ground" between Buddhists and Christians. This point of contact has been encouraged by the response to Buddhism of Thomas Merton and other Christians of monastic contemplative traditions. One wonders, in hearing proposals of this sort, whether the Buddhists understand that contemplative meditation is not a central practice in at least some Christian traditions. Protestantism, in general, has never been markedly contemplative in either its theory or in its practice. If the dialogue is to be confined to the monastic orders and their lay adherents, then it needs to be labeled clearly as dialogue, or rather as a partnership conversation, between Buddhist monasticism and Christian monasticism. Only in that qualified sense is it a dialogue between Buddhism and Christianity. Any dialogue that assumes from the Buddhist side that Christianity is also centered in the practice of meditation will be monological in the same sense as one in which Christians assume that Buddhists really worship the same God as Christians, albeit under another name.

A truly dialogical relationship has no other purpose than itself. Dialogue is the end of dialogue. It is common to justify dialogue as something that helps us to understand ourselves better, as something that contributes to our own growth and maturity. Whereas change in the form of growth is something that one might well hope and expect from a dialogical relationship, it cannot be its prime purpose. To attempt dialogue for what we can get out of it is too egocentric an attitude. If the dialogue partner is viewed primarily as the instrument for my growth, then he or she is a means for my own fulfillment rather than one who is loved for his or her own sake. With that view of the other, I am still bound up in what, in Buber's terms, is an I-It relationship. A relationship that is entered into for the results it will bring, whether it be the conversion of the other or our own growth, is still in the realm of monologue.

The choice between dialogue and monologue in our relationships is not a choice between two methods, one of which will get us the better results. If there is an imperative to dialogue it is, in Kant's terms, a categorical and not a hypothetical imperative. In more biblical terms, the choice between mono logue and dialogue is the choice between death and life. If to be human is to live in community with fellow human beings, then to alienate ourselves from community, in monologue, is to cut ourselves off from our own humanity. To choose monologue is to choose death. Dialogue is its own justification.

We need to explore the ethical question that is implied here somewhat further. The question of whether there is an imperative to dialogue needs to be answered on at least two levels. On the level of activity, the question is whether, assuming that one is able, one ought to enter into a dialogical conversation with a particular group. In some cases, as we have already seen, the question will never really have to be asked because the preconditions for a dialogical relation are not present. We can recall here Cobb's examples of Nazism and the Ku Klux Klan. We need to be cautious here, however, because the history of interreligious encounter is filled with examples of groups pronouncing the disability of other groups for dialogue prior to any attempt to establish a dialogical relationship.

Theologies of isolation and hostility are particularly prone to this. One can appropriately make the judgment that another group is incapable of openness and good faith only after dialogue has at least been attempted. Assuming that a dialogical relationship with another tradition has not been ruled out, then the question of whether one ought to enter into a dialogical conversation with the other tradition is a practical question that has to deal with the ordering of priorities. The community must decide which of its many dialogical conversations has the greatest claim on its resources.

The claim that is being made in this chapter, however, concerns the ethics of the dialogical relationship. Put bluntly, the claim is that dialogical relationships are either impossible or they are obligatory. They are impossible when two communities are incapable of mutual trust and openness. In all other cases, dialogical relationships are obligatory.

This categorical claim needs some qualification. As a categorical claim, namely that dialogue is either impossible or obligatory, all that has been said is that one compromises the dialogical relationship if one attempts to justify it by its results. A relationship that is justified by what one can get out of it is not a dialogical relationship. That is not to say that there are not benefits that result from dialogue. There certainly are benefits. The claim that dialogue leads to growth, to deeper self-understanding, is certainly true. To enter a dialogical conversation for these reasons, however, is to compromise the dialogical relationship from the start.

To speak of the dialogical imperative is an abstract and "secular" way to speak of the commandment of neighborly love. To love one's neighbor as oneself is to be in a dialogical relationship with one's neighbor. More specifically, the New Testament puts the command in striking form: we are to love our neighbors *as God has loved us.*[1]

To move directly from the commandment to the dialogical imperative, however, is to make certain assumptions that need to be spelled out. One can justify nondialogical relationships from the commandment if one makes certain ideological assumptions about God or about love. In particular, it is possible to make certain authoritarian assumptions about God combined with a neurotic view of how a parent loves a child through controlling his or her every move, in order to think of love as doing "what is best" for one's neighbor. "What is best," of course, is defined by us, not by our neighbor.

When the New Testament speaks of loving our neighbor as God has loved us, it is not speaking of this kind of neurotic "love" and it is not using a monarchical model of God or Christ. It is the servanthood of Christ, not his "Kingship" that is the paradigm that lies behind the commandment. What the commandment refers us to is the self-giving, the kenosis of Christ, which in its openness and vulnerability leaves us free to respond either by entering a dialogical relationship with Christ (by responding to the openness and vulnerability of Christ with openness and vulnerability of our own) or by remaining closed and unresponsive.

There is here an important issue here for evangelical Christianity, and one that ought not to be minimized. The question, put abstractly, is how the self-giving of Christ is made known to people of other religious traditions and how their response is invited. We need to defer that question to a later chapter. Here we simply need to note that it would be inconsistent with the commandment to use the dialogical relationship which Christ calls us into with himself to justify a monological relationship with one's neighbor.

The commandment to love one's neighbor as Christ has loved us translates for the Christian into the dialogical imperative, the imperative to seek dialogue and to be open to dialogue whenever and from whomever it is offered.

The fact that dialogue may be possible infrequently, ambiguously, and fragmentarily does not mitigate the dialogical imperative. It is a fact of the human situation that openness and vulnerability are not always reciprocated. One cannot force one's neighbor into dialogue. One cannot prevent the neighbor from using our openness as an opportunity to manipulate us. Those risks are part and parcel of vulnerability. One has to be ready to accept crucifixion if one is to love as Christ loved us.

Theologically, this can be interpreted in terms of human fallenness. Christian tradition, especially in the West, has attempted to deal with the reality of human existence by speaking of "original sin" or, in Reformed Protestant theology as "total depravity." In interreligious dialogue, these terms need careful interpretation, but the traditional doctrines are intended to point to the fact that although we may know the good, our capacity to do the good is never entirely pure. Our best intentions may be frustrated by our own self-alienation or by the alienation that is structurally present in the world we live in. The fact that we may not succeed in doing the good does not qualify the categorical imperative to do it.

The fact of our finite freedom, as Paul Tillich attempts to restate the traditional doctrines of human nature, needs to be clearly recognized in relation to the dialogical imperative. A dialogical relationship does not happen easily. It is a precarious relationship, vulnerable to being converted to monologue without notice. On both sides there must be a will to dialogue. Yet even more than will is required. Even with the best will on both sides, dialogue may not happen. As Buber says, the I-Thou relationship requires both will and grace.

Christian discipleship, then, involves a call to unconditional openness to the neighbor. As with most calls to discipleship, we can find reasons for not following, and, even when we do follow, the quality of our obedience leaves much to be desired. Our difficulty, however, is with the ambiguity of our lives, not with the ambiguity of the call. The call to dialogue, to open, trusting and loving relationships with the neighbor, is clear and unambiguous. Dialogue needs no justification outside itself.

14

Cosmic Dialogue

To consider dialogue as a categorical imperative, as a relationship that is its own purpose, is to ascribe something of an unconditional character to it. One of the implications of this is that there is no situation in which dialogue is not an appropriate relationship. There may indeed be situations in which dialogue is so undercut by our own resistance to dialogue that the relationship is never established. However, there is no situation in which we escape from the dialogical imperative. If we are not in dialogue, we ought to be.

That conclusion calls into question many of the traditional attitudes about mission. Mission, as I use the term here, refers to the calling of the Church by God into the world. The question of mission is the question of the nature of that call. When God calls the Church into the world, what does God intend that the Church do there? How does God intend the Church to relate to the world?

The types of relationship that we have described as isolation, hostility, competition, and partnership have all been expressed, at one time or another, as a theology of mission. In a theology of isolation, for example, the world is seen as a realm of darkness. The mission of the church is to take light into darkness, knowledge to the ignorant. This view has been prominently represented in the literature of the missionary movement of the last few centuries.

A theology of hostility is expressed in the missiology of many sectarian movements. The world is the enemy of God. It is itself not capable of redemption but is doomed to ultimate destruction in the final victory of God. God, through the work of people of genuine faith, calls people out of the world. The mission of the Church, therefore, is a rescue mission. The community goes into the world in order to pull people out of it.

A theology of competition stresses that Christians have to live "in" the world, but that they ought not to be "of" the world. This is a theology of the "church-" type rather than the "sect-" type of religious community. If people have to live in the world, they nevertheless have to be wooed away from the temptations of "worldliness." The Church is thus called into competition with the world, the stakes being the ultimate loyalty of individual souls.

A theology of partnership represents the world positively. As the creation of

God, the world is good. The goodness of the world and the call of the Church are synonymous. Consequently, the world can be allowed—indeed *ought* to be allowed—to set the agenda for the mission of the Church. The mission of the Church is to name and to support the signs of God's activity in the world.

Each of these theologies of mission can appeal to the Bible for support. The fact is that the Bible, particularly the New Testament, uses the term "world" ambivalently. On the one hand, the world is God's creation and the object of God's love. On the other hand, the world is evil, the organized body of human and spiritual rebellion against God. An adequate biblical doctrine of the world would have to deal carefully with the tension that is inherent in this ambivalence. If one wants to pick and choose, however, it is not difficult to find biblical support for quite different theologies of mission. One can color the world white or black as one chooses. One can appeal to the Bible for confirmation of one's choice.

Most theologies of mission have tended to treat mission as a monological activity. The Church, it is argued, is called to preach, to teach, to heal, and to baptize.[1] These are primarily activities in which the Church does something to and for the world. The Church gives, the world receives. The Church speaks, the world listens.

In all of that, there may be a reciprocal listening of the Church to the world. But the listening is justified primarily because it helps the Church to speak better. The Church listens in order that it might understand better what the world hears when the Church speaks. When the Church proclaims the Gospel, it wants the world to get the message right. If the world understands the wrong thing when the Church says "God," the Church needs to know about it. By listening to the world, the Church improves the way that it tells the world what the world needs to hear.

This approach to mission assumes, in one way or another, that the Church knows about the world prior to the Church's engagement with the world. The Church may not know the details. Therefore, the Church has to listen. The decisive things, however—what the world needs, and the answers to the needs of the world—the Church knows a priori. In missions, the Church has the diagnosis and the prescription for the world's ills all ready to administer. The diagnosis is ignorance and the answer is revelation. The diagnosis is sin and the answer is redemption in Christ. The diagnosis is oppression and the answer is liberation.

With this view of the mission of the Church, dialogue can be no more than one aspect, among others, of the things that are done by the Church in mission. Dialogue has to fit in with other priorities. Whatever priority dialogue is given at some point or other, we must go beyond dialogue and engage in activities that are usually described by the words "witness" or "proclamation." Dialogue is granted a certain value but, it is argued, the Church fulfills its mission only as it is faithful to its mandate to witness and proclaim.

The problem with this approach is not with its insistence that the Church has a mandate to witness and proclaim. One could deny this only at the price of a radical falsification of the biblical record. The problem lies with the assumption that insofar as one witnesses and proclaims one must step out of the dialogical relationship. The problem is that the view ends in an exaltation of monologue.

Consider this statement from the Lausanne Occasional Papers, which represent a conservative evangelical perspective on mission:

> The use of dialogue in reaching people has to be carefully considered. This method paves the way for a sharing of experiences, and provides an opportunity for frank interchange in conversation. It provides an atmosphere in which both parties can understand each other, and creates a mutual bond of friendship and appreciation. However, it must not end there. It must lead to proclaiming Christ as Lord.[2]

In spite of the limited appreciation of dialogue expressed in this statement, mission is assumed to be ultimately and primarily monological. Dialogue is seen as a means, not of meeting people but of "reaching" people. The point of reaching people, of course, is expressed in the last sentence. At some point in the relationship, dialogue must be superseded by "proclamation." The representatives of other religious communities must be told that Christ is Lord.

Against the representation of dialogue as a means to evangelization, we can only reiterate that a conversation in which one of the parties has an ulterior motive cannot be genuinely dialogical at all. This kind of conversation may prove to be very effective in preparing the ground for evangelization. But it is not genuine dialogue.

The Lausanne papers reflect what is best described as a moderate conservative evangelical point of view. However, the assumption that witness and proclamation are "beyond dialogue" is represented by the World Council of Churches as well. The World Council is concerned to make witness as dialogical as possible. In the final analysis, however, witness and dialogue are distinct activities:

> Witness may be described at [sic] those acts and words by which a Christian or community gives testimony to Christ and invites others to make their response to him. In witness we expect to share the good news of Jesus and be challenged in relation to our understanding of, and our obedience to that good news.
>
> Dialogue may be described as that encounter where people holding different claims about ultimate reality can meet and explore those claims in a context of mutual respect. From dialogue we expect to discern more about how God is active in our world, and to appreciate for their own sake the insights and experiences people of other faiths have of ultimate reality.[3]

The Vancouver Assembly of the World Council of Churches attempted to resist any position that would make witness and dialogue into antithetical activities. The report repeatedly refers to mutual witness and to the hearing by Christians of the witness of those of other traditions. Nevertheless, the monological assumptions of this definition of witness cannot be hidden. Dialogue consists of mutual exploration of visions of ultimate reality. In witness, by contrast, we "speak" and then we listen to the feedback that pertains to what *we* have said. In the World Council report, witness and dialogue are interrelated. But at some point, the Church in mission must go beyond dialogue and engage in a different activity called "witness."

The problem stems in part because witness and dialogue are conceived as "activities" or "events." As an activity alongside other activities, dialogue is relative and must take its place as one priority among many. So long as we tie the words "dialogue" and "witness" to specific types of "happenings," then the problem of finding a place for both activities will persist.

When we speak in terms of the dialogical imperative, however, we are talking of attitude and relationship rather than activity. What is universally binding is not a life of going from one "dialogue" to the next "dialogue" but entering into relationships marked by openness, honesty, and the search for understanding.

Dialogue is not just an activity among other activities. It is, first and foremost, a fundamental relationship into which we are called with our neighbor. Unless dialogue is selective—that is, unless we are called into dialogical relationships with some people but not with others (which could only be the case if dialogue were not universally binding)—we must say further that dialogue is a fundamental relationship with the world to which we are called.

If this is the case, we ought not ask how we balance dialogue and witness as activities that are sometimes complementary, but often in competition among the priorities of the Christian community. The question ought rather to be what "witness" and "proclamation" mean within a dialogical mode of being and within a dialogical relationship with the cosmos. We have allowed "witness" and "proclamation" to be defined from the perspective of ideologies that exalt monologue. The difficulty may not be with the mission to which the Church is called by Jesus Christ, but with ideologies that have limited our vision of what witness and proclamation can be.

The question that is raised by these ideologies is whether proclamation and witness are antithetical to dialogue. The question is serious because, as we have admitted, proclamation and witness are clearly activities that are constitutive of the mission of the Church. If the Church's mission is what is mandated in scripture, and it is difficult to see how it could be other than what is mandated in scripture, then an adequate missiology has to make sense of witness and proclamation as central to the calling of the Church in the world.

Whether we are conservative evangelicals or liberal universalists or something in between, we tend to have a stereotype of witness and proclamation as a kind of arrogant dogmatic pronouncement. We imagine these activities as a kind of announcement of a truth that no amount of listening to others could ever touch. The person who hears our witness or proclamation has the option of accepting what we pronounce or of remaining in his or her ignorance and error.

Having named that stereotype, let us set it aside to focus on the way that the concepts of witness and proclamation meant in the apostolic and postapostolic church. What we find there is an understanding of mission—of witness and proclamation—that is not as clearly opposed to dialogue as our modern stereotype would suggest.

Both witness and proclamation in the New Testament are forms of storytelling. The witness reminds us of a witness in a court of law. The witness is a person who tells a story that, when supported by other witnesses, creates a presumption of the credibility of the story. Similarly, proclamation is the telling of the kerygma. The kerygma has the form of a story. It tells of God's activity in the history of Israel and in the person and work of Jesus Christ.

Witness and proclamation are very closely related activities. If they are to be distinguished at all, both are still fundamentally the telling of the Christian story.

Why, we need to ask, does it seem that witness and proclamation are antithetical to dialogue? As a genre, story is not at all monological. Story is an invitation to the listener to participate actively. Story both engages the imagination of the listener and leaves the listener free. It is difficult to imagine a dialogue that does not include the sharing of stories.

The tension that we perceive between witness and dialogue is closely related to the fact that we tend not to associate witness and proclamation with storytelling. Rather, the words connote to us images of the lawgiver, the moralizer, the dogmatist. In our operative images of witness and proclamation, the hearer is not left free. A story does not attempt to prescribe the response of the hearer, even though it does invite response. Legalism, moralism, or dogmatism tends to narrow acceptable responses to "yea" or "nay," "obey" or "disobey," "accept" or "reject."

The story is told of a Zen Master who, on hearing a passage from the Sermon on the Mount, remarked that "Whoever said that is not far from Buddhahood." It is important to see in that remark a positive response to the proclamation of the Gospel. It is not the response that the Christian community would sometimes like to prescribe for its proclamation. Nevertheless, it is a positive and genuine response to the very question that Christians have generally identified as central to the proclamation: "Who do you say that I am?"[4]

The necessity for proclamation to invite response does not exclude proclamation or witness from dialogue. In dialogue, we always respond to each other's stories. In genuine dialogue, this response is reciprocal. If the Zen Master is able to respond to Jesus, so Christians, hearing the Buddhist story, also respond to the Buddha. Furthermore, our response to the Buddha is not without its impact on the way that we tell the Christian story. Our telling of our stories in witness and proclamation is never as monological as we often make it appear.

In Christian tradition the witness, the proclamation, is the telling of a shared story. The way that the story is told is not fixed or eternal. It has been told differently as the secular and historical context has changed. The story has always been told in dialogue with the world. Despite some appearances, the storytelling of the Christian community has not and cannot be abstracted from the continuing dialogue of the community with its worldly context.

The proclamation of the Christian community developed a relatively fixed form quite early in the history of the tradition. This form is probably best summarized in the Apostles' Creed. The story tells of God's creation of the world, of God's dealings with Israel, of the ministry, death, and resurrection of Jesus, and of the culmination of history at the end of time. This relatively fixed form of the story obscures the fact that the telling of the story has differed markedly at different times and in different places. Some elements of the story are glossed over. Other elements are given special emphasis. The concrete form that the story takes in any telling of it reflects the ongoing dialogue in which the storyteller is engaged with his or her world. That the kerygma assumed a Hellenistic dress in the early Church is not so much a compromise of its Hebrew roots (as is often intimated). The Hellenistic form that the telling of the story took in the early Church is the result of the necessary dialogue of the early Christian community with its own time and place.

The dialogue with other religious communities is only a special case of the dialogue with the cosmos into which the Church is called. This point cuts two ways. First, it implies that the Christian community, like other religious communities, cannot see its mission as primarily confined to the sphere of "religion" (whatever that might mean). Secondly, it implies that our relationship with other religious communities is not qualitatively different from our relations with the various secular communities whom we encounter in the world we live in. Let us look at each of these points in a bit more detail.

First, then, the Christian community (like other religious communities) cannot construe its mission as narrowly "religious." In the present historical context, the suggestion that religious communities should "stick to" religion is expressed in the light of religious communities' involvement in important political and economic issues. The view proposed suggests that as governments are in the political sphere and corporations are in the economic sphere, so religious communities are in the religious sphere. Consequently, this view suggests, religious communities should not become involved in questions of justice, peace, and human rights.

This view is generally rejected by religious communities. The issue, for the religious communities, is not ideology but "faithfulness." This is true whether the religious community be represented by the World Council of Churches, the Moral Majority, or the Shi'ite Muslim community in Iran. Faithfulness, for religious people, typically involves an ongoing concern for and dialogue with the wider community of the world.

The sense of religious communities as having a secular mission implies that the question of dialogue with other religious communities does not hinge on the fact that the various religions are in "the same business." The case for dialogue with other religious communities is *not* based on the assumption that all religious communities have something in common: namely, religion. Religious communities don't simply engage in dialogue with each other. The call to dialogue is a call to dialogue with the whole world.

The second point, that the relation between religious communities is not qualitatively different from the relation between a religious community and its secular neighbors, provides the corollary to the first point. In many situations, there is an attempt to do just that—to prescribe one type of relation between "church" and "world" and another type of relation between "church" and "church." In many churches, for example, the relation between church and world (i.e. the secular community) is viewed as fundamentally dialogical. In the World Council of Churches, and in many of its member denominations, it is a fundamental dialogical stance in relation to the world that underlies its political critique of peace and justice issues.

The dialogical openness to the secular community that is characteristic of the World Council of Churches is not necessarily applied to the relation of the churches to non-Christian religious communities. While dialogue with secular communities may be affirmed, other religious communities may be viewed as competitors. The dialogical relationship affirmed as appropriate in the secular realm is suddenly reversed when we enter the realm of religion.

The view that religious communities have a special interest in dialogue with each other and the view that religious communities exist in essential competition with each other are both rooted in the same assumption. Both views assume that religious communities have "something in common" with each other that they do not share with nonreligious communities. Both views assume that religious communities are "in the same business" and that, consequently, either "partnership" or "competition" are the appropriate relationships between them.

Against that view, we have here been proposing the view that mission is fundamentally dialogue with the world. This view is proposed as an interpretation of Christian mission without, thereby, precluding the possibility that it might also be true of other religious communities.

To describe mission as cosmic dialogue does not rob mission of its critical element. If we take the secular dialogues of the churches as an example, we can understand this point clearly. In the sphere of human rights, of justice and of peace, the churches have time and time again been drawn into critiques of racism, of classism, of sexism, of militarism. The point to be understood is that these critiques do not issue from an arms-length relationship with the world. On the contrary. It is precisely as Christians have embraced the world, in openness and concern, that the Christian critique of the injustice of the world's structures has developed.

A dialogical relationship with the world does not entail the suspension of judgment. Neither does it preclude anger. Dialogue places judgment and anger in a new context. Dialogue may require that we search for a new style of expressing ourselves on those occasions when we may need to speak a negative word. What we need to insist is that prophetic criticism ought not to be a pretext for avoiding the dialogical imperative.

15

Dialogue and Theology

Several commentators on interfaith dialogue have, in recent years, argued that a fundamental shift in Christology is required for an adequate Christian theology of religion. John Hick,[1] Alan Race,[2] and Paul Knitter[3] each make this case in parallel arguments. Each argues in his own way that traditional doctrines of the person and work of Jesus Christ imply that other faith traditions are somehow lacking in their knowledge or experience of God. Traditional Christology, it is implied, makes it difficult, if not impossible, for Christians to recognize the integrity and spiritual validity of other faith traditions. They argue that a shift from a Christocentric theology to a theocentric theology is necessary for the development of a theology of religions that is genuinely open to other faith traditions.

It is not my purpose here to criticize the alternative Christologies advocated by Hick, Race, and Knitter. The point I wish to question is whether such a conversion in Christology is a precondition to dialogue on the part of Christian churches in general or of Christian theology in particular.

Race identifies three different types of Christian attitudes to other religions: the exclusivist, the inclusivist, and the pluralist. The first sees genuine knowledge and experience of God confined to Christian faith. The second grants that genuine knowledge and experience of God may exist in other traditions but holds that the fullness of that knowledge and experience of God can be found only in Christianity. The pluralist view represents the different traditions as different expressions of a knowledge and experience of God that is common to many traditions.

Race's analysis, at least in its broad outlines, is shared by Hick and Knitter. In Hick, the analysis tends to be simplified in his concern to distinguish the "Copernican" and "pre-Copernican" attitudes to other religious traditions. Knitter's analysis is more complex, taking into account more of the subtle differences between theological positions. All would share the conviction that a fundamental shift is required for an adequate Christian theology of religions and for a genuine openness of Christian communities to dialogue. It is that conviction, rather than the "theocentric" Christologies that they advocate, that I want to question here.

At a purely practical level, the strategy advocated by Hick, Race and Knitter does not appear to be a promising one. The great majority of Christian churches have regarded themselves as rooted in Nicene orthodoxy. In Western Christianity, the test of Christological orthodoxy was the formula of Chalcedon, the understanding of Jesus Christ as "very God and very man, without confusion and without separation." The Christologies advocated by Race, Hick, and Knitter are presented as alternatives or as corrections to traditional Chalcedonian orthodoxy. Put that way, the case for dialogue with non-Christian traditions will be seriously compromised in the eyes of the mainstream of Christian believers. Forced to choose between interfaith dialogue and traditional Christological orthodoxy, the churches can be predicted to choose what they perceive to be a faithful Christology, one that passes the test of the Chalcedonian formula. The case for interfaith dialogue will be better made, if it is possible, if it proceeds from, rather than in opposition to, what the churches have traditionally understood faithfulness in Christology to involve.

That point, as I have said, concerns strategy. It is not an argument against the substance of the theocentric position. Hick, Race, and Knitter imply that the preferable strategic option—that of affirming traditional Christological doctrine—is not a possible one. They argue that traditional Christological orthodoxy ties Christians to a patronizing and nondialogical attitude to other religious traditions. The only possible way to an adequate theology of religions and to a genuinely dialogical attitude to other religious traditions is through a radical departure from traditional Christological doctrines. If true, it should be noted, the position would confirm the worst fears of Christian critics of dialogue. It would be heard as an argument *against* positive interfaith relationships. This objection is typically phrased like this: "If interfaith dialogue requires us to be less than faithful to Jesus Christ as that faithfulness has always been understood in the church, then, surely, Christians ought not to involve themselves in interfaith dialogue."

Let us move to the center of the issue. Hick, Race, and Knitter reject Christologies that describe Jesus as the revelation of God in terms like "unique," "final," or "decisive." In one form or another, traditional Christologies have described Jesus as "the unique and decisive revelation of God." In Race's analysis, "unique" is the term that underlies the exclusivist view. "Decisive" is the problem term in what he describes as the inclusivist position (which, in our terms, is the competitive, "preparation for the Gospel" position). One who believes that Jesus is the "unique and decisive" revelation of God cannot, according to the theocentrists, acknowledge the validity and integrity of the knowledge of God in non-Christian traditions.

My problem with the theocentrist argument is this. The statement "Jesus is the unique and decisive revelation of God" is a statement about Jesus. It is *not* a statement about Muslims or Hindus or Buddhists. Simply on the level of logic, a statement about Jesus cannot become a statement about Buddhists or Hindus or Muslims without another premise. Something has to connect a Christian confession about Jesus with a negative judgment about other religious traditions. Taken by itself, a Christology—even a very particularist high Christology—does not carry the implication that members of non-Christian traditions live, in some important sense, outside the providence of God.

The "theocentric" argument sees Christological orthodoxy, the Christology that stresses the individual Jesus as the unique incarnation of God, as the root problem preventing Christians from fully appreciating, and entering into dialogue with, people of other religious traditions. The argument infers that there is a direct connection between our statements about Jesus and our statements about the spiritual condition of non-Christian people. The Christology is represented, at least in part, as the "cause" of an undesirable attitude to other religious traditions. In contrast to that view of Christology as the cause of exclusivism, I have attempted to develop an understanding of interfaith relations that sees our theories about other religious traditions as rooted in our social contexts. Thus, it is true that a particular Christology can be used to support a particular relationship with another religious tradition. In this sense, a traditional Christology lends itself to supporting a relation of isolation or competition. It is easy to characterize people of other traditions as ignorant by invoking the belief that Jesus Christ is the unique revelation of God. However, it is quite another thing to assume that our Christological belief is the *source* of the ideology of isolation. The problem here is not a religious belief that is held by Christians about Jesus Christ. The problem is that, in an isolated community, this Christological belief lends itself to the ideology of the community.

Christological affirmations are statements about Jesus, not about people of various religious faiths. To infer the spiritual state of non-Christians from these confessions would require some additional premise.

I have tried to argue that often the additional premise is an ideological one. An exclusivist theology of religions can be the result of uniting a high Christology with the ideological convictions that those outside our community live in a sphere of ignorance.

The additional premise is not always ideological. It may be theological. To say that "Jesus is the ultimate and decisive revelation of God" is not quite to say that "If, and only if, I know Jesus then I know God." Conservative evangelicalism, as represented in the Lausanne Occasional Papers, for example, finds it necessary to go beyond the claim that Jesus Christ is the ultimate and decisive revelation of God. It must also specify that human salvation is dependent on *explicit* faith in Jesus Christ. It is that qualification, and not Christological orthodoxy alone, that is necessary to establish the exclusivism that the Lausanne papers represent. This qualification, however, is not the necessary consequence of a high Christology. It is a distinct and additional theological premise in conservative evangelical missiology.

The issues here are complex and subtle. We need to observe, though, that there have long been differences among Christian theologians about the significance of the individual's belief in Jesus. Are we saved by what we believe? Some theologies—and this is particularly true, for example, of revivalistic evangelicalism—hold that a positive reception of Jesus by the individual is indeed necessary for salvation. Other theologies are more universalistic, holding in various ways that knowledge of God or salvation is conveyed by Jesus outside the sphere of Christian belief. Wherever there is knowledge of God, wherever there is salvation, there is the sign of the presence of Jesus.

The theocentrists argue, however, that an opening to people of other faith involves a radical revision of traditional Christology. One could, I suppose, try to make the case that traditional Christology was the product of a community that needed support for an ideology of isolation or even of hostility. While the Christology may lend itself to those ideologies, I doubt that a study of the historical origins of traditional Christological doctrine could succeed in making the case very effectively. Rather, it has been religious motives dealing with tensions within the community, not ideological motives dealing with rivalries with non-Christian communities, which have been decisive in shaping traditional Christology. The issue for Athenasius in his criticism of the Arians, for example, was the reality of our salvation, not the question of how Christians were to relate to their pagan neighbors at the beginning of the Constantinian era. Athenasius argued, in effect, that unless Christ was fully divine, he could not have the power to effect the salvation that the Gospel claims for him. Similarly Karl Barth, who advocated what many consider to be an extreme Christocentrism in theology, was concerned about tensions within the Christian community, not about how Christians were to relate to the other religious traditions of the world. To Barth, Christocentrism was protection against the self-deification of humanity, a tendency that, in Barth's eyes, had its logical conclusion in the cooperation of the German Church with Nazi totalitarianism.

The theocentrists are certainly correct that the high Christology of an Athenasius or of a Karl Barth is by no means the whole story in the history of Christian thinking about Jesus Christ. What is objectionable is not their opting for an alternative to the traditional doctrine but their suggestion that advocates of the traditional doctrine are not prepared for genuine dialogue and an adequate theology of religions. They are naturally critical of those who would want to convert their non-Christian neighbors. But the position they espouse really does demand a religious conversion of the vast majority of Christians themselves. Hick appeals for a conversion to a "Copernican" view of God. Knitter, with a certain insensitivity to Protestant traditions, urges a conversion to a "catholic" view with which even many Catholics will have difficulty.

At the strategic level, an approach to Christology like the one suggested by John Cobb would seem to be preferable to that suggested by the advocates for "theocentrism." In his work on Christology, Cobb develops a position that is carefully stated in order to meet the criteria for Christological orthodoxy that are represented by the formula of Chalcedon.[4] Cobb argues that a faithful Christology, even given traditional criteria of faithfulness, is not inconsistent with an open dialogical relationship with other religious traditions. This is a quite different approach to that of Hick, Race, and Knitter, who argue that such an open relationship with other religious traditions requires a fundamental break with at least some traditional criteria of faithfulness in Christology.

The thesis I have attempted to advance here is that the theological agenda for Christians who are concerned with our relation with other religious traditions needs to focus on a theology of dialogue, not on a new doctrine of God or a new doctrine of Christ, or a new doctrine of salvation. Dialogue—genuine dialogue—ought not to require any prior conversion on either side, other than a conversion to, and a commitment to, the relationship of dialogue itself.

It would be naïve to expect that Christians, entering into dialogue with other traditions, would not experience fundamental changes in their religious beliefs. Genuine dialogue with other traditions may be expected to have a profound effect on the way that our faith is understood—that is to say, on our theologies. Our doctrines of God, our doctrines of Christ, our doctrines of human nature, our ecclesiologies, our doctrines of salvation—all of our doctrines may be expected to be radically recast as a result of our participation in genuine dialogue. These changes, however, are the *consequence* of dialogue, not a precondition for dialogue.

The approach of John Cobb is again instructive. Cobb[5] points to what he calls "creative transformation" as the hope of the emerging dialogue between Christians and Buddhists. The road to creative transformation is through dialogue, whether or not it is actually "beyond dialogue," as Cobb suggests. Whether or not the particular transformations that Cobb anticipates are likely as the result of Buddhist-Christian dialogue is quite debatable. As Christians enter into dialogue with Buddhists, we can be sure that transformation in our understanding of God, transformation in our understanding of human nature, transformation in our understanding of salvation, will follow.

In order for me to enter into dialogue with Buddhists, I do not need to change my Christology any more than I expect Buddhists to become theists. Insofar as my Christology is indeed a Christology (and not a covert ideology of isolation or hostility), it need not be an obstacle to dialogue. All that I need to believe, for genuine dialogue to begin, is that Buddhists are not out of touch with reality. Once the fundamental sanity of Buddhists is granted, it follows that there is some point to dialogue, to understanding how the world looks through Buddhist eyes.

As a Christian, I am likely to persist in my belief that Buddhists are wrong about God. I am not likely to adopt their belief that the existence or nonexistence of God is irrelevant to the spiritual quest. Nevertheless, the Buddhist critique of theism will inevitably cause me to examine and reexamine my own theistic assumptions. As a result of coming to understand reality as seen by Buddhists, my own doctrine of God will be transformed.

To speak of Buddhists or Muslims or Hindus as not being out of touch with reality is to say something that others have attempted to say in ways that carry too much theological freight. Some people attempt to speak of dialogue as an exchange of truths, as if dialogue were a trading of truths, some of which are possessed by Christians, some by Buddhists, some by Hindus. To speak of truth as if it were a quantifiable commodity does not help to describe what actually happens in dialogue. This notion of different truths that are known in different religions leads some to speak of there being different revelations of God in different religious traditions, the existence of Buddhists "truths" being evidence of a Buddhist "revelation." The fact that the very notion of "revelation" is a Christian category that has little or no place in Buddhist self-understanding is conveniently ignored.

What one discovers in dialogue is not different "truths" as much as it is different perspectives on the the same reality. The one reality with which we deal is the reality of being human in the world. As I integrate Buddhist perspectives, Hindu perspectives, and traditional native perspectives into my own perspective as a Christian, my understanding is transformed.

I am suggesting that the theological agenda in interfaith relations needs to focus on a theology of mission rather than on Christology. A theology of mission is nothing else than a theological understanding of the relationship between the Church and the world. That relationship will take the form of a theology of isolation, a theology of hostility, a theology of competition, a theology of partnership, or a theology of dialogue.

Obviously, the question cannot be resolved by proof texts. Any of these theologies can be "justified" by a selective use of scriptural texts. In each case, the "proof texts" are not trivial ones. Each of the theologies can point to themes that are central to the message of the Bible as the basis for their theology of mission. Our justification of dialogue on the basis of neighbor-love is, in this sense, just as selective as the use of the Bible by the other theological ideologies.

In the logic of Christian thought, a theology of mission is understood to be one aspect of an ecclesiology, a doctrine of the Church. The theology of the Church is, in turn, linked to Christology, the being of the Church being understood in analogy to the person and work of Jesus Christ. In raising the question of a theology of dialogue, then, we are led back to Christology, but not in the same way as the question of dialogue leads back to Christology in the "theocentric" approach. The theocentric approach attempts to move directly from Christology to a theology of the world. It assumes that a Christian theology of the world is a direct implication of a theology of the person of Jesus Christ. I have already argued that the connection is ideological as well as logical, that statements about Christ are not in any direct way statements about the world in general or about non-Christian people in particular. Let us look, however, at how ecclesiology mediates between a Christology and a theology of the world.

Typically, the relation of the Church to God and the relation of the Church to the world is understood in analogy to the relation of God to the world in Jesus Christ. In its relationship to God, the Church is understood as an aspect of the human side of the divine-human relationship. In relation to the world, the Church is understood in analogy to the divine side of that relationship. Simply put, in its missiology, the Church asks "How does God relate to the world?" Having answered that question by the example of Jesus Christ, the Church asks how it can follow that example in its dealings with the world.

Mission is understood in terms of analogies with God's ways of relating to the world. These analogies are stated in very different ways by different theologians. The formal analogical relationships between Christology, ecclesiology and missiology are, however, typical of a wide range of theological approaches.

In a rough, but not too misleading sense, the analogy works like this: The Church understands itself as being at the same time a human institution and a divinely instituted reality. The human and divine "sides" of the Church are "like" the human and divine natures of Jesus Christ. The doctrine of the Church is understood as deriving from an *analogy of relationship*. When we extend the analogy to a theology of mission, then, we need to say that the relationship between the Church and the world is "like" the relationship between the divine and human natures of Jesus Christ.

The theocentric approach as it has been represented here attempts a "Christology from below." That is, it begins with the human situation and the human Jesus and attempts to speak of Jesus as the Christ, of the relation between Jesus and God, from that perspective. The alternative approach is a "Christology from above." This approach begins with the mystery of the Incarnation, from the divine humanity of Jesus Christ, and attempts then to speak of the human situation. Both approaches have long theological traditions behind them. It is not my intention to become involved in a debate between the two approaches.

Given the critique of the theocentrists, it would seem that a "Christology from above" would be the more difficult basis for a theology of dialogue. I have argued that dialogue ought not to involve a conversion in Christology. We need to look at the "hardest case," then, to see how a theology of dialogue might be derived from a "Christology from above."

Let us start with the Chalcedonian formula, the benchmark test for Christological orthodoxy, at least in Western Christianity. The Council of Chalcedon marked the culmination of a series of false starts in attempting to state an adequate doctrine of the person of Jesus Christ. These false starts have been immortalized in the names of some of the major Christological heresies: Arianism, Appolinarianism, Nestorianism, and so on. The formula of Chalcedon solved the problem, not so much by defining an adequate Christology as by naming the problems that an adequate Christology might avoid. The formula asserts two natures, divine and human, in the one person of Jesus Christ. It goes on to say, essentially, what that union of divine and human was *not*. The union is "without confusion." The divine and human natures are not to be construed as if they were merged into an alloy that is neither divine or human. The union is "without separation." Jesus is not to be seen as a spiritual schizophrenic, sometimes human, sometimes divine. We cannot abstract a pure divinity or a pure humanity from Jesus. The divine and human are both present in every aspect of both the person and the work of Jesus Christ. The Chalcedonian formula does not tell us how this union of two natures in one person might be possible. It simply asserts the union against the various "false starts" that had been attempted as answers to the problem.

Let us, then, start by accepting the major assertion of Chalcedon, namely, that Jesus Christ is fully human and fully divine in a unique and decisive way. What might follow from that for a theology of dialogue?

Since we are dealing with analogy, we need to ask this: Given that the divine and human are in intimate relationship in Jesus Christ, how can we construe that relationship? What does the "mystery of the Incarnation" tell us about the relationship between God and the world? Is the relationship between God and the world one of isolation, of hostility, of competition, of partnership, or of dialogue?

I will rule out two of those possibilities at once: hostility and competition. In the Chalcedonian definition, the humanity of Christ is not a fallen humanity. There is no sense that the humanity of Jesus is at war with his divinity or that the divine and human natures are locked in a struggle to see which will get the upper hand. The temptation stories of the Gospels are instructive here. They are designed to show the absence of competition or hostility between the divine and human in Jesus, in spite of the fact that it may have seemed at times in the interest of the human nature of Jesus to initiate such a struggle.

Is the relationship between the divine and the human one of isolation? Is the divine Jesus all-knowing and the human Jesus in darkness and ignorance? This construal of the relationship would seem to require a separation of the two natures of the type forbidden by Chalcedon. We would say that when Jesus displayed weakness, when he cried, when he was tired, he was being human. When he showed strength, authority, and power he was being divine. This is precisely the type of spiritual schizophrenia that the Chalcedonian formula would rule out.

That leaves partnership and dialogue as our models for understanding the divine-human relationship in the Incarnation. A partnership model would hold that the relationship between the divine and human is based on something that the divine and human have in common. This position is at least a possible one. There is a strong tradition in Christian theology that would interpret the concept of the *imago dei*, the image of God in humanity, as the basis for the union of the divine and human in Jesus Christ. In this theory, human nature has at least the potential for uniting with divine nature. In short, the world is potentially divine.

The dialogical relationship, however, may be even more appropriate for construing the divine humanity of Jesus Christ. This model would understand the divine and human in the relation of an I to a Thou. Each nature is open to the other. In Jesus, to put it simply, God learns what it is like to *be* human. The humanity of Jesus, conversely, is open to the divine perspective. In Jesus, God and humanity are free to address and to be addressed, to respond in openness and love. At every moment, Jesus *is* this dialogue. His life and work are continual expressions of the perennial dialogue between God and world.

When the divine-human relationship is transferred by analogy to ecclesiology and to a theology of mission, then, we would seem to have two basic options. Either we see our solidarity with the world in terms of a natural solidarity that all humanity has with God, or we see the Church as called into the same intimate dialogue with the world that is represented by the divine-human dialogue in Jesus. In either case, our exploration in high Christology has not resulted in any warrant for the exclusivist position that the advocates of theocentrism are so anxious to avoid.[6]

The affirmation of the presence of God among peoples of other religious traditions, then, does not require a critique of particularist doctrines of revelation, nor does it require a Christological conversion. What it does require is a strong critique of the ideologies that guide how Christologies and doctrines of revelation are applied. It requires a missiology that is firmly rooted in our doctrines of God, Christ, and human nature. It requires a missiology that is for the world, but that is critical of the ideologies of the world—whether those ideologies have the origins in ourselves or in others.

NOTES

1. THE IDEOLOGY OF ISOLATION

1. Stephen Neill, *Christian Faith and Other Faiths: The Christian Dialogue with Other Religions* (London: Oxford University Press, 1961), 1.

2. Will Herberg, *Protestant—Catholic—Jew: An Essay in American Sociology* (Garden City, N.Y.: Doubleday, 1956).

3. William Carey, *An Enquiry into the Obligation of Christians to Use Means for the Conversion of the Heathen* (Leicester, 1792), 13.

4. Reginald Heber, "From Greenland's icy mountains," *The Hymnary of the United Church of Canada* (Toronto: United Church Publishing House, 1930), Hymn 256.

5. Barth addresses the question of religion in *Church Dogmatics*, I/2 (Edinburgh: T. & T. Clark, 1956), 228–361. Barth's position is discussed in Chapter Six.

6. John Cobb, *Beyond Dialogue* (Philadelphia: Fortress Press, 1982), 18–21.

7. With the term "liberation theology," I am referring to a popular attitude more than to a formal theological movement. These comments are not intended to describe any particular theologian or group of theologians. "Liberation theology" is a term that is used very loosely, and it is that loose use of the term that is reflected here. It refers to an attitude or perspective that would identify the most serious faith issues of our time with issues of justice and power.

It should be noted, however, that a number of "third-world theologians," particularly Asians, have been insisting on the importance of interfaith questions for the contemporary theological agenda.

2. THE IDEOLOGY OF HOSTILITY

1. Martin Luther, *Concerning Rebaptism: A Letter of Martin Luther to Two Pastors* (1528) in *Luther's Works*, Vol. 40 (Philadelphia: Muhlenburg Press, 1958), 232.

2. Martin Luther, *The Keys* (1530) in *Luther's Works,* Vol. 40, 348–349.

3. Martin Luther, *On the Jews and their Lies* (1543) in *Luther's Works*, Vol. 47 (Philadelphia: Fortress Press, 1971), 164.

4. William R. Goetz, *Apocalypse Next* (Beaverlodge, Alberta: Horizon House, 1980), 191.

5. Marius Baar, *The Unholy War: Oil, Islam and Armageddon* (Nashville: Thomas Nelson, 1980).

6. I use the terms "dispensationalist" and "premillennialist" interchangeably. Dispensationalism is a theory that interprets different parts of scripture as being given by God for different periods of history or "dispensations." Premillennialism is a particular belief about the nature of the "last days" and the second coming of Christ. In fact, dispensationalists are generally premillennialists. The opposite is not necessarily true.

There are forms of premillennialism that are not dispensationalist. The popular form of premillenialism today is, however, a dispensationalist one.

7. Barr, 37.

8. Ibid., 24.

9. Ibid., 31.

10. Ibid., 170.

11. Ibid., 148–9.

3. THE IDEOLOGY OF COMPETITION

1. Cf. Freidrich Schleiermacher, *The Christian Faith* (Edinburgh: T. & T. Clark, 1928), 31–39.

2. Kenneth Boa, *Cults, World Religions, and You* (Wheaton, Ill.: Victor Books, 1977).

3. Ibid., 6.

4. Ibid., 7.

4. THE IDEOLOGY OF PARTNERSHIP

1. John Hick, *God Has Many Names* (London: Macmillan, 1980), 45.

2. Ibid., 48f.

3. The image of the "Copernican Revolution" is central to Hick's understanding of the significance of his position. The Ptolemaic universe was geocentric. Everything in the cosmos revolved around planet Earth. The Copernican universe removed Earth from the center and in its place put the sun, around which Earth and the other planets revolved.

To Hick, a particularistic view of God (i.e., God as revealed in a particular religion) is "Ptolemaic," while a universalist view (which places God at the center in place of the particular religion) is "Copernican." The analogy would seem to imply that a particularistic view of God is a form of ignorance, in the same way that the Copernican theory defined the Ptolemaic theory as ignorance.

4. Cf. also John Hick (ed.), *The Myth of God Incarnate* (London: SCM Press, 1977).

5. THE SCOPE OF THE TYPOLOGY

1. H. Richard Niebuhr, *Christ and Culture* (New York: Harper and Row, 1951).

2. In speaking here of "powers," I do not intend to mystify abstractions like "philosophy" and "religion." Rather, I want to make the point that terms like "philosophy," "religion," and "technology" refer to something real, but they cannot be reduced to names of simple communities. They also refer to distinct methodologies and languages that permeate human communities in very complex ways. In speaking of "powers," I am attempting to avoid either sheer abstraction of the concepts on the one hand, or a misplaced concreteness on the other.

6. RELIGION AND FAITHFULNESS

1. Cf. Alan Race, *Christians and Religious Pluralism* (London: SCM Press, 1983), 11ff.; Paul Knitter, *No Other Name?: A Critical Survey of Christian Attitudes toward the World Religions* (Maryknoll: Orbis, 1984), 70ff.

2. Cf. John Cobb, *Beyond Dialogue* (Philadelphia: Fortress Press, 1983), 15–21.

3. Karl Barth, *Church Dogmatics*, I/2 (Edinburgh: T. & T. Clark, 1956), 280–361.

4. Ibid., 340ff.

5. Race, 16.

6. Barth, 284–291.

7. Ibid., 325–361.

8. Barth's discussion of the methodological implications of the first commandment is found in a 1933 lecture, "Das Erste Gebot als Theologisches Axioms," in *Theologis-chesche Fragen und Antworten* (Zollikon: Evangelscher Verlag, 1957).

9. The logical point at stake here is a simple one. If one starts with the attributes of two versions of God, how can one establish that they are versions of the *same* individual? Without knowing all the attributes, one has neither necessary nor sufficient grounds to make the identification. But one would have difficulty knowing *all* the attributes of God.

10. I am indebted to Schubert Ogden for this way of phrasing the issue.

11. Karl Barth, *Church Dogmatics*, IV/3, First Half (Edinburgh: T. & T. Clark, 1961), 116–117.

12. Ibid., 126.

13. Ibid., 127.

14. Ibid., 128.

7. FAITHFUL AGNOSTICISM

1. The word "could" needs to be emphasized. There are Christians who engage in Buddhist meditation and who include the bow to the Buddha nature as part of their practice. Whether one can do this in good conscience is a personal decision. There is no theoretical reason why it cannot be done. The relevant questions are: What does bowing before an image mean for you? (integrity) What does bowing before an image mean for others? (witness)

2. Idolatry is the unique problem of the monotheist. I suspect that Muslims and Jews feel this tension even more acutely than do Christians and that Protestants are more sensitive to the problem than are Catholics. The intensity with which the tension is experienced will reflect (a) the stress placed on the transcendence of God by the tradition and (b) the interpretation of the commandment against images.

3. Cf. Karl Rahner, *Theological Investigations*, Vol. V: Later Writings (London: Darton, Longman and Todd, 1966), 118–132.

4. Judgments like these are *experiential* judgments that cannot be universalized. A Christian might legitimately say, "I have known Buddhists who have exhibited the fruits of the Spirit." One cannot say, "Buddhism, like Christianity, is a revelation of God." The latter is a universal judgment. It reveals its a priori nature by the fact that, in Kantian terms, it goes beyond the limits of any possible experience.

8. TWO PHILOSOPHERS OF DIALOGUE

1. Martin Buber, *Between Man and Man* (Macmillan, 1947), 7.

2. Martin Buber, *I and Thou* (New York: Scribner's, 1958), 8.

3. Ibid., 7.

4. Martin Buber, *Between Man and Man*, 22–23.

5. Buber, *I and Thou*, 75.
6. Ibid., 80.

10. DIALOGUE AS NEGOTIATION

1. Visser t'Hooft, *No Other Name* (London: SCM Press, 1963).

11. DIALOGUE AS INTEGRATION

1. Cf. Paul Tillich, *Systematic Theology*, Volume I (Chicago: University of Chicago Press, 1951), 22–28.
2. Cf. Ludwig Wittgenstein, *Philosophical Investigations* (Oxford: Basil Blackwell, 1958).

12. DIALOGUE AS ACTIVITY

1. John Cobb, *Beyond Dialogue*, 10.

13. THE DIALOGICAL IMPERATIVE

1. 1 John 4:19.

14. COSMIC DIALOGUE

1. Cf. Matthew 28:19—the "Great Commission."
2. *Christian Witness to Hindus*, Lausanne Occasional Papers, Number 14 (Wheaton, Illinois: Lausanne Committee for World Evangelization), 22.
3. *Gathered for Life: Official Report, VI Assembly, World Council of Churches, Vancouver, Canada, 24 July–10 August 1983*, ed. David Gill (Geneva: W.C.C. Publications and Grand Rapids: Eerdmans, 1983), 40.
4. Matthew 16:15.

15. DIALOGUE AND THEOLOGY

1. John Hick, *God Has Many Names: Britain's New Religious Pluralism* (London: Macmillan, 1980).
2. Alan Race, *Christians and Religious Pluralism: Patterns in the Christian Theology of Religions* (London: SCM Press, 1983).
3. Paul Knitter, *No Other Name?: A Critical Survey of Christian Attitudes toward the World Religions* (Maryknoll, N.Y.: Orbis, 1984).
4. John Cobb, *Christ in a Pluralistic Age* (Philadelphia, Westminster Press, 1975).
5. John Cobb, *Beyond Dialogue* (Philadelphia: Fortress Press, 1982).
6. It will be no secret to my readers that my own preference is for an understanding of mission as *dialogue* with the world rather than as *partnership* with the world. Theologically, however, that issue turns on issues of what we understand by the "image of God" and of human fallenness. It does not follow from the exercise in high Christology that I have attempted here.

Index